TPI New Testament Commentaries

General Editors
Howard Clark Kee   Dennis Nineham

The Pastoral Epistles

TPI New Testament Commentaries

These paragraph-by-paragraph commentaries have been written by modern scholars who are in touch with contemporary biblical study and also with the interests of the general reader. They interpret the words of the New Testament for the twentieth century in the light of the latest archeological, historical and linguistic research and are neither over-simplified nor abstruse and academic.

TPI New Testament Commentaries

The Pastoral Epistles

I and II Timothy, Titus

J. L. HOULDEN

SCM PRESS
London
TRINITY PRESS INTERNATIONAL
Philadelphia

227.83

First published 1976 by Penguin Books Ltd
This edition first published 1989

SCM Press   Trinity Press International
26–30 Tottenham Road   3725 Chestnut Street
London N1 4BZ   Philadelphia, Pa. 19104

British Library Cataloguing in Publication Data

Houlden, J. L. (James Leslie, 1929–)
   The Pastoral Epistles: I and II Timothy, Titus.
   1. Bible. N.T. Pastoral Epist Commentaries
   227'.8307

   ISBN 0–334–01327–5

Library of Congress Cataloging-in-Publication Data

Houlden, J. L. (James Leslie)
   The Pastoral Epistles: I and II Timothy, Titus/J. L. Houlden
      p. cm.—(TPI New Testament Commentaries)
   Includes the Revised Standard version text of the Epistles.
   Reprint. Originally published: Harmondsworth : Penguin, 1976. (The
   Pelican New Testament commentaries).
      Bibliography: p.
      Includes indexes.
      ISBN 0–334–01327–5 : $14.95
      1. Bible. N.T. Pastoral Epistles—Commentaries. I. Bible.
   N.T. Pastoral Epistles. English. Revised Standard. 1976.
   II. Title. III. Series.
   (BS2735.3.H68   1989)
   227'.83077—dc20   89–35801

334 01327 5 (cased)
334 01326 7 (paper)

Printed in Great Britain by
Richard Clay Ltd, Bungay, Suffolk

For my pupils at Cuddesdon

Contents

Commentary

Acknowledgements

The author wishes to thank the General Editor of the Pelican Commentaries, Dennis Nineham, Warden of Keble College, Oxford, for his invitation to write this commentary; Patricia Richardson for making the indexes; Peter Strange for reading the proofs; and pupils and friends for their companionship and encouragement while he was writing.

References, Abbreviations
and Technical Terms

The biblical text used is the *Revised Standard Version*.

The titles of the books of the Bible receive their customary abbreviations. Biblical references are given by chapter and verse, and where necessary also by section of verse; thus Heb. 13^a means the first half of verse 3 of chapter 1 of the Epistle to the Hebrews.

Articles in periodicals are cited by the abbreviated title of the periodical, followed by the volume number and/or its date, then the page number. Standard collections of documents are referred to by the editor's name or an abbreviated title, followed by volume and/or page numbers.

A & G   *A Greek-English Lexicon of the New Testament*, edited by Arndt and Gingrich, Chicago and Cambridge University Press, 1956.

BJRL   *Bulletin of the John Rylands Library.*

Charles   *Apocrypha and Pseudepigrapha of the Old Testament*, vols. I and II, edited by R. H. Charles, Oxford University Press, 1913.

ECW   *Early Christian Writings*, translated by Maxwell Staniforth, Penguin, 1968.

Hennecke   *New Testament Apocrypha*, vols. I and II, edited by E. Hennecke and W. Schneemelcher, English translation edited by R. McL. Wilson, Lutterworth Press, 1963.

JAC   *Jahrbuch für Antike und Christentum.*

JBL   *Journal of Biblical Literature.*

JTS   *Journal of Theological Studies.*

LCC   *Library of Christian Classics.*

LXX   The Greek version of the Old Testament, the Septuagint, so called because it was believed to be the work of seventy-two translators working independently, and by a miracle producing an identical version in seventy-two days. It differs considerably from the Hebrew text on which our English translations are based.

MS(S)	Manuscript(s).
NEB	New English Bible, New Testament, Oxford University Press, 1961.
NTS	*New Testament Studies.*
RSV	Revised Standard Version of the Bible, Nelson, 1952.
TDNT	*Theological Dictionary of the New Testament*, Grand Rapids, 1964–74.
Vermes	*The Dead Sea Scrolls in English*, edited and translated by G. Vermes, Penguin, 1962.
ZNTW	*Zeitschrift für Neutestamentliche Wissenschaft.*

Introduction

What are the Pastoral Epistles? They are three writings, first called by that title by Aquinas in the thirteenth century, then, in modern times, by the German scholar, Anton, in the first half of the eighteenth century, but always placed together in the New Testament, and clearly, as even a quick reading shows, belonging together in a set. Until the beginning of the nineteenth century, everybody believed them to be the work of Paul and they had an assured place among the apostle's writings in the New Testament. That is almost true, but not quite: there are one or two signs that in the second century they were not always included in the collection of his works, and, if our view of them is right, there must have been a number of people who, in the first days of the life of these writings, were perfectly aware that they had come from another pen than his. Now most scholars take them not to be authentic Pauline writings.

If there is at least a strong chance that they are not by Paul, why do we continue to pay attention to them? In the first place, they have always been in the New Testament, to whose authority, in a variety of ways, the Christian Church has deferred so powerfully, and there they remain. For their size, these writings have had an enormous influence in Christian history. A glance at the ordination services in the Church of England's *Book of Common Prayer* will show how strongly they have coloured traditional concepts of the Church's ministry. These writings were seen as giving the instructions of Paul on subjects hardly touched in the other writings. They portrayed a more ecclesiastical Paul, a Paul with whom bishops and other Church authorities of later days could easily identify. Here he wrote of things which deeply concerned them and on which they were glad of his guidance.

They have had a role which has been partly edificatory and partly controversial. As the ordinals of the churches show, they have helped to provide ideals for Christian clergy. And it is no accident that when ideals of priestly life and a sense of Church authority were revived in the Church of England in the nineteenth century, people appealed constantly to these writings. Cuddesdon Theological College, founded in devotion to these ideals in 1854, took I Tim. 6^{20} ('Guard the deposit') as its motto, inscribing it even upon its chamberpots! The emphasis in the Pastoral Epistles on discipline and moral earnestness appealed strongly to the aspirations of Victorian churchmen. Untroubled, most of them, by doubts about authorship, these men were gratified to find in Paul, hitherto generally regarded as the patron rather of the basic tenets of Reformation Protestantism, such strong support for their aims.

Not only edificatory but also controversial. These writings speak of the government of the Church with a clarity and fullness lacking in the other letters attributed to Paul. And they seem to support a system remarkably like that which became general in the Church from at least some time in the second century and remained virtually unchallenged until the Reformation; that is, the rule of churches by a bishop, supported by a group of elders (readily translated into priests) and deacons. In the period of the Reformation, the Calvinist churches and some of the Lutheran churches abandoned this system, generally by necessity rather than desire, and there was controversy about the scriptural basis of the forms of ministry they adopted instead. The Pastoral Epistles can bear more than one interpretation on this matter, and they played an important part in discussion of the question. Since the nineteenth century too, both in the Tractarian revival in the Church of England and in ecumenical discussion, the question of church government, and in particular the place of bishops in the Church, has been of central importance. Again, these writings have been appealed to, with varying degrees of wisdom and sense.

Many Christians engaged in the consideration of these questions would nowadays be a little wary of reckoning to find clear guidance for the present-day Church in the institutions reflected in the writings of the New Testament. They are more aware that, whatever the similarities, there are vast differences of situation and outlook between the little congregations of those early days and the Christian bodies of today. 'Timothy' and 'Titus', followers of Paul, the alleged recipients of these letters, simply cannot be equated without qualifications with bishops, superintendents, moderators, or any other officers of the twentieth-century Church. The move from finding these writings edifying to regarding them as demanding imitation in all respects was a false one, quite apart from its unforeseen complexity.

But there is another reason why these writings are still worth studying, even if we take them not to be by Paul. If they were not by him, then they were certainly by somebody who thought it worth writing in his name. What sort of person could he be? Why should anyone in the early Church think of doing that? And what does it tell us about the mentality and circumstances of such a man? Was he a reprehensible forger, or were his motives more respectable? Or is moral judgement not quite the best line to adopt in estimating these works? If they were not written by Paul, but, we may suppose, after his time, when was that? How soon did they appear, and why, at that particular time, was there pressure to assume Paul's mantle? All these questions are worth pursuing; and if we can answer them, one important result follows. We shall have lengthened, perhaps considerably, our perspective on the early Church; we shall have extended the period on which the New Testament as a whole throws light into the years after Paul's death, perhaps, as we shall see, into the first half of the second century; we shall have discovered something of the interests and anxieties of certain Christians of that time, reflected obliquely through these pseudo-Pauline letters. We shall also – and this is equally important – be able to see Paul himself more clearly. On any showing, it is not in all respects easy to see the Paul of the undoubted letters and the Paul of these writings as all of a piece. So we can now improve the focus.

For such reasons alone, these writings are worth studying. They take us on from the earliest Christian times into the next period – that of the Church's acclimatization to the world. In one sense that period is still with us. Yet many of the more vigorous elements in the churches today would reject any such ideal. Even if they do not share Paul's expectation of a speedy end to the present world-order they have much more sympathy with his sense of sitting light to human institutions and the encumbrance of social life than with the somewhat humdrum and conventional aspirations which seem to underlie these writings despite their occasionally more inspired moments. So many who read them today find them less immediately edifying than their great-grandfathers did. It is not simply because their authenticity as Pauline is rejected; rather, Christian sensibilities have changed.

These writings, then, tell us things not only about the early Church but also about ourselves. And if they arouse us to impatience with their often prosaic attitudes, our duty is to enter into the situation in which they arose and ask ourselves how Christians could better have reacted to the problems then before them. If they spoke as Paul did not speak, if they put different qualities first and favoured different policies, this was partly because they faced different questions. In one form or another, these questions – of identity and authority – always face the Church on earth. One use of the Pastoral Epistles is to stop us ignoring them out of mere impatience and because we feel that Christians have paid them enough attention in the past. In the end, the questions had better be answered than banished from sight.

AUTHORSHIP

This question is fundamental. We can make little headway towards answering some of the interesting questions mentioned above until we clear our minds about the matter of Pauline authorship.

The reasons for questioning it are of two kinds: style and content. Neither in vocabulary and literary techniques nor in atmosphere and teaching is it plausible to suppose that these writings come from the same pen as the main body of Paul's letters. The first matter lends itself to statistical demonstration, the second is more one for discrimination. We take the view that both point firmly in the same direction.

A complicating factor is the presence in these works of a number of passages which look patently Pauline, whatever may be said about the rest. They consist of notes, dealing with the movements and activities of various associates, friends and opponents of Paul (e.g. II Tim. 4^{9-21}), together with a small amount of more personal material, written by the apostle, so it appears, shortly before his death (II Tim. 4^{6-8}). Anyone inclined on other grounds to decide that Paul did not write the letters must be given pause by these passages.

We shall examine these matters in turn.

Style and form
It is worth trying to decide whether to take these writings as three distinct but related works or to see them as a single, tripartite composition. At first sight, the former view is self-evidently right: they

are of uneven length; as far as destination is concerned, the first two are a pair and the third stands on its own; with regard to circumstance, II Timothy shows Paul in prison, the other two letters do not.

But there are some signs that the writer was setting out to produce a single work in the form of a triptych. In general tone, I Timothy and Titus stand together against II Timothy. The two former are much less personal. Unlike II Timothy, they make no attempt to arouse either sympathy or admiration for Paul. In that writing, we feel the same warmth towards Paul as in the accounts of the trials in the later chapters of Acts and in a passage like Acts $20^{17ff.}$, with which indeed there are interesting points of contact. To be more precise, it is not only tone but subject matter which unites I Timothy and Titus. Both cover the same range of topics: the evil of heresy; the form and character of office in the Church; the conduct required of other groups in the Church; statements of Church doctrine. They appear thus:

Heresy	Office		Other Groups	Doctrine
	form	conduct		
I Tim: 1^{3-11}	$3^{1-10,12f.}$	$1^{18f.}$	2^{8-12}	$1^{15f.}$
$1^{19f.}$	5^{17-22}	4^{11-16}	3^{11}	2^{3-6}
4^{1-9}		$6^{11f.}$	5^{1-16}	3^{16}
6^{3-5}		$6^{20f.}$	$6^{1f.}$	4^{10}
				6^{14-16}
Titus: 1^{10-16}	1^{5-9}	2^{1}	2^{2-10}	1^{1-3}
3^{9-11}		3^{8}	$3^{1f.}$	2^{11-14}
			3^{14}	3^{4-7}
II Tim: 2^{14-18}		1^{6-8}		$1^{9f.}$
2^{23}		$1^{13f.}$		2^{8}
3^{1-9}		2^{1-7}		4^{1}
$4^{3f.}$		3^{14-17}		4^{8}
		4^{2}		
		4^{5}		

Much of II Timothy belongs in a category found there alone – the bearing and conduct of 'Paul' himself as a suffering apostle: 1^{11-12}; $2^{9f.}$; $3^{10f.}$; 4^{6-18}. Its range is partly narrower than, partly different from, the rest.

The analysis under these headings is by no means perfect – there are overlaps and there are passages capable of more than one allocation. But it is sufficient to bear out our point. A number of comments suggest themselves:

1. Much of the material in II Timothy, which can reasonably be put under the headings shown, is nevertheless much more related to the person and life of 'Paul' himself than most of the comparable material in the other writings, e.g. 1^{6-8}; $2^{17f.}$ (but cf. I Tim. $1^{19f.}$); 4^8.

2. II Timothy shows no sign of thinking in terms of the various categories (which we have somewhat tendentiously distinguished as 'office' and 'other groups') into which the Christian 'household' can be divided. The other writings do.

3. The strongest affinity of the second and third doctrinal passages in Titus is not with I Timothy but with II Tim. $1^{9f.}$ and 4^1. So the relatively meagre doctrinal element in II Timothy is not without connections elsewhere.

Assuming then that the work is not Pauline, we may see it as a three-sectioned composition, giving the writer's message, mostly in plain, straightforward terms, partly didactic, partly hortatory, in the first and third sections, with the second section designed to appeal to the reader's loyalty and sympathy rather than to admonish and instruct him. If this is what was in the writer's mind, then it gives us a first reason for seeing the personal apparatus, including the letter format, as contrived. It has been imposed upon the underlying plan.

Or it may be that I Timothy and Titus were planned as alternative statements of the same points and originally stood side by side, the present order being the result of a rearrangement designed to put the two letters addressed to Timothy together. If this were the case, one result would be that there would be even more reason than otherwise for thinking that in our writer's eyes the schemes of Church officials in the two writings are not significantly different (cf. pp. 74 and 142). The idea might in that case have been to show Paul as having spread this wholesome teaching to places as far apart as Ephesus and

Crete: it was his universal provision. II Timothy would then, as before, play the 'backing up' role of arousing Pauline loyalty.

Whatever the precise truth in this matter, there are clearly grounds for thinking these writings were originally planned as a whole. On any showing, they all exhibit roughly the same range of concerns: when we come to the commentary itself, we shall find that almost everything needing comment in Titus can partly be dealt with by reference to passages in the two earlier letters!

It should be recognized that there is nothing surprising, in the light of the conventions of the time, in a writer using the form of letters to present works which are nothing of the sort. In this case, there was the primary motive, that Paul in his lifetime was known to have communicated by means of letters and imitation was a means of commendation; but even without this, the form of the letter was an acceptable medium for presenting moral and other instruction of the kind we find in these writings, especially in I Timothy and Titus. Not surprisingly the best known examples are from the realm of government and administration: compare the exchange between the Emperor Trajan and the younger Pliny early in the second century.*

But the view taken in this commentary is that these writings were pseudonymous. That too is part of the conventional apparatus of the time. In the New Testament itself, II Peter and Jude are almost universally agreed to be written in the name of rather than by the men whose names they bear, and other works, I Peter, James, Ephesians, are all strong candidates for this status.†

Many of those who wish to retain an element of Pauline authorship, while at the same time seeing that the differences from the unquestioned epistles are too great to be explained by the apostle's growing older or writing in new circumstances, opt instead for the view that in the making of these letters an amanuensis was used and had perhaps a great deal of freedom. But quite apart from the fact that this takes no account of the indications of post-Pauline circumstances, it is on any showing remarkable that in these writings, as distinct from others (compare for example Rom. 16^{22}; I Cor. 16^{21}; Gal. 6^{11}), there is no

*See *The Letters of the Young Pliny*, Betty Radice (ed.), Penguin, 1963, p. 260ff.; also *The Letter of Aristeas*, Charles, vol. II, p. 83ff.

†K. Aland, 'The Problem of Anonymity and Pseudonymity in Christian Literature of the First Two Centuries', *JTS*, 12, 1961, p. 39ff.

sign whatsoever of the use of this method (cf. p. 32). The hypothesis is shaky.

If our inquiry so far leads us to regard these writings as literary productions rather than genuine letters, and for that reason alone unlikely to come from the pen of Paul, what can we learn from other approaches to their style and form?

First, their vocabulary has two notable features. In the first place, it is un-Pauline. In the second place, it has close affinities with that of the Christian writers of the late first and early second centuries, the so-called Apostolic Fathers.* Both are matters of statistical inquiry, but the former leads to surer conclusions: if Paul wrote our three pieces, then he was certainly being unlike his usual self, and we may at best (see above) infer the use of an amanuensis, after the common practice of the ancient world. The affinity with the Apostolic Fathers requires more circumspect handling: can we really be so certain that their vocabulary is characteristic of Christian writers of precisely those few decades and no others, or, to be exact, none earlier? Have we a sufficient quantity of Christian (and usefully related other) literature of the period to make judgements of this kind? At best we can say that, as far as it goes, the evidence in this respect points to a date for the writing of the Pastoral Epistles later than the lifetime of Paul; and the argument will be useful if other evidence apart from that of mere word-usage points the same way.

The evidence on this question is set out in the works of P. N. Harrison.† Some of the more important figures given by Harrison are these: of the 848 words (other than proper names) which form the vocabulary of the Pastoral Epistles, 306 do not occur in any of the other epistles attributed to Paul; 175 do not occur in any other New Testament writing. The Pastorals and Paul share 542 words, but 492 of these occur also in other New Testament writings. Of the 175 words found only (within the New Testament) in the Pastoral Epistles, sixty-one occur in the Apostolic Fathers and in addition

---

*See in ECW or vol. I of *Library of Christian Classics*, London, 1953, or the classical edition by Bishop J. B. Lightfoot, London, 1891.

† *The Problem of the Pastoral Epistles*, Oxford University Press, 1921, which he annotated and extended in *Paulines and Pastorals*, Villiers, 1964. See also K. Grayston and G. Herden, 'The Authorship of the Pastorals in the Light of Statistical Linguistics', *NTS*, 6, 1959.

twenty-nine others in the slightly later group of second-century Christian writers known as the Apologists. Harrison's books* must be consulted for the full details, though in the commentary we shall, as we proceed, note many of the more striking examples of word usage. Even this brief array of statistics is enough to show that the argument for non-Pauline authorship is not ill-founded and that there are grounds, even on the basis of vocabulary alone, for finding links with later writings. Harrison's second book (cf. especially ch. 3) takes the comparison further, by examining links with non-Christian writings of the same period (the end of the first century and the first three quarters of the second). Sixty-one of the seventy-eight words which, by the time of this book, Harrison reckoned were absent from the rest of the New Testament, the Apostolic Fathers, and the Apologists, occur elsewhere, notably in pagan writers like Dio Chrysostom, Plutarch and Epictetus, who lived during the period A.D. 50–150. There are also striking connections with the somewhat earlier Jewish writer Philo† and with Josephus and the LXX.

A more specific link has been explored recently by C. F. D. Moule‡ and, in more detail, by A. Strobel§ – that with Luke-Acts. The connection both with Luke the writer and (supposing them to be identical) Luke the man has been canvassed for many years, first by H. A. Schott in 1830.

The link with the man suggests itself from II Tim. 4^{11}: 'Luke alone is with me.' This has been taken both as a clue revealing Luke as the amanuensis who wrote up (perhaps with a large measure of independence) II Timothy at least – and therefore, because of the overwhelming stylistic homogeneity, also I Timothy and Titus. (Because the reference is in the third person, it has also been taken, for example by J. Jeremias, as actually excluding Luke's part in writing these letters!)

But even those who cannot be convinced by this reference alone or who regard the remarks at the end of II Timothy as fictitious or

---

*See also R. Morgenthaler, *Statistik des Neutestamentlichen Wortschatzes*, Zürich/Frankfurt am Main, 1958.

†cf. P. N. Harrison, *Paulines and Pastorals*, Villiers, 1964, p. 135ff.

‡ *The Birth of the New Testament*, A. & C. Black, 1962, p. 220ff. and 'The Problem of the Pastoral Epistles; a Reappraisal', *BJRL*, 47, 1965.

§'Schreiben des Lukas?' *NTS*, 15, 1969, pp. 191–210.

who are not disposed to identify the Luke of Paul's entourage (Col. 4[14]) with the writer of Luke-Acts must recognize many affinities of vocabulary, style and thought between those works and the Pastoral Epistles.

First, vocabulary. Strobel has shown that there are some thirty-seven words which, within the New Testament, occur only in Luke-Acts and the Pastorals – a figure which comparable counts show to be high. In addition, twenty-nine shared words occur only rarely in the rest of the New Testament. It may be of some interest that no less than eleven of the thirty-seven words appear in speeches ascribed to Paul in Acts. While the advocate of Pauline authorship might here find some comfort, one might rather feel that if the same writer were responsible for both sets of works and if he were writing with a certain Pauline self-consciousness in the Pastorals (on any showing, there is considerable dependence on Paul's writings), he would carry this particularly into Paul's speeches.

The shared words include some of central importance in the Pastorals, others much more marginal. In the former category come words of the *eusebeia* ('godliness') group which, apart from five appearances in II Peter (a work with numerous signs of similar date to the Pastorals), are confined to these works. These words are particularly symptomatic of the religious air breathed in these writings (cf. p. 63ff.). So is *sōphrosunē* ('modesty'), confined to I Tim. 2[9,15] and Acts 26[25]. Words of the *philarguria* ('love of money') group occur only in I Tim. 6[10]; II Tim. 3[2]; Luke 16[14]; and Heb. 13[5]; and the theme is a major concern of Luke, as well as our writer in I Tim. 6 (though it is fair to say that it is a commonplace of contemporary moral teaching).

In the area of style and expression: the two groups of writings share an unusually frequent use of the impersonal verb *dei* ('must'): thirty-three times in Luke-Acts, eight times in the Pastorals. Both have uses of the preposition *epi* with *pisteuō* ('believe'); only in I Tim. 1[12]; II Tim. 1[3]; and Lk. 17[9] do we find *charin echō* for 'I thank'. In Lk. 12[11] *archai* and *exousiai* are used for 'rulers' and 'authorities', differing from the Matthean parallel (10[18]); Tit. 3[1] uses the same two words. For the link between II Tim. 3[11] and Acts 14, cf. p. 126.

Both writings have what could be called a 'saviour christology'. Alone among the Gospels (apart from John 4[42]), Luke has this title

(2^{11}); and it occurs twice in Acts, once in a Pauline speech (5^{31}; 13^{23}). Furthermore, it is also applied to God – Lk. 1^{47}. In the Pastorals, the use of the title for both God and Jesus is strikingly frequent, cf. p. 47f. We should also notice the language about the 'saving' of a 'sinner' in Lk. $19^{7,10}$, and compare the formulation of Jesus' mission in these terms in I Tim. 1^{15}. Though this understanding of Christ's work was a natural one in the Hellenistic Christianity of this time (cf. p. 48), the occurrence of it in precisely these two sets of writings, which also share so much in their conception of moral priorities and piety, is certainly impressive. Any reader of Paul's farewell speech in Acts 20 and then of II Tim. 4 is bound to feel that the same writer may be at work, expressing thoughts of particularly deep concern to him. In that speech above all we may see Paul handing over that 'deposit' of faith which 'Timothy' in Ephesus, on a par with the elders of Ephesus in this respect, whatever title he may have borne, was to guard (I Tim. 6^{20}).

This view has been attacked, partly on the grounds that the Pastorals owe too much to the Pauline epistles for them to come from the author of Acts, who, with few exceptions, shows himself rather remote from Paul.* However, there are grounds for an opinion which may seem to be a hedging of bets: first, there are signs in the Pauline speeches in Acts of something like that use of Pauline passages as models but without a deep appreciation of Pauline thought which we also find in the Pastorals (cf. p. 51f.; and see Acts 13^{39}, using Paul's common *dikaioō*, 'justify'; Acts 14^{15} and I Thess. 1^9); second, the writer of Luke-Acts was capable of adapting his style to his context, as the birth stories in Lk. 1–2 and the septuagintally influenced speeches in the early chapters of Acts show clearly†; so that the hypothesis we are considering simply widens the range of his versatility.

While this attempt to identify the author of the Pastorals cannot be regarded as proven, any more than others which work on other grounds (cf. p. 42), it certainly helps to define further the world to which all the writings under discussion belong and to place these writings after the lifetime of Paul. When we turn more explicitly to considerations of thought and circumstance, then we may again find

*cf. N. Brox, 'Lukas als Verfasser der Pastoralbriefe?', *JAC*, 13, 1970.
†H. F. D. Sparks, 'The Semitisms of Acts', *JTS*, I, 1950, pp. 16–28.

that Luke-Acts and the Pastorals belong to the same milieu, both in the history of the early Christian Church and in the world of thought of their time.

Ethos and teaching

Words are not simply items to be counted, they also have meanings. When we turn to the sense of the words, we find that the results of the statistical inquiries are confirmed. Those results are negative and positive: first, these writings are unlike Paul; second, they are like Church writings of a few decades after his death and like some pagan writers of the same period. They also have similarities with Jewish writers of the same or an earlier period, notably Philo.

They are unlike Paul. In this respect, they are different from Ephesians, also widely believed to be a pseudonymous letter issued under the name of Paul.* That work is saturated with Paul's vocabulary and phraseology. In our writings, however, as in Paul's speeches in Acts, there is a notable lack of both Pauline words and Pauline thought. Harrison† lists eighty-eight words lacking in the Pastorals but found in four or more of the other Pauline epistles (including Ephesians). They include such important doctrinal terms as: spiritual, wisdom, cross, uncircumcision, son, abound, preach the gospel (*euaggelizomai*), tribulation, body, boast.

In other cases, our writer has the Pauline sense but a different word to express it. For 'thank' (I Tim. 1¹²; II Tim. 1³), he has not Paul's common *eucharisteō*, but *charin echō*; for Christ's expected return, not *parousia*, but *epiphaneia*.‡

The Pastoral Epistles can use this latter word not only for Christ's second coming but also for his first (cf. II Tim. 1¹⁰), a twin concept not found in Paul. The Pastorals make no explicit reference to the death of Christ, though his trial appears in I Tim. 6¹³ and the saving effect of his death is referred to in I Tim. 1¹⁵; 2⁶; Tit. 2¹⁴. These last references are all, however, somewhat formal, and the reader may feel that they do not spring from the heart of any creative theological pattern. This area of belief, in other words, does not occupy the same

---

* cf. J. L. Houlden, *Paul's Letters from Prison*, Penguin, 1970, p. 235ff.

† *The Problem of the Pastoral Epistles*, Oxford University Press, 1921, p. 31ff.

‡ cf. p. 101 and P. N. Harrison, *The Problem of the Pastoral Epistles*, Oxford University Press, 1921, pp. 28–30.

place for our writer as it did for Paul, in whose works it is crucial. (Since the comparison with Luke has been made, we may note how little that writer feels at home with technical theological terms in describing Jesus' death in the Gospel, and how he ventures such language only once in his Pauline speeches, Acts 20²⁸, where the wording is not that of our writer, though the sense is close to that of Tit. 2¹⁴.)

There is no reference to the resurrection of either Christ (except, by bare allusion, II Tim. 2⁸) or the Christian (except to deny it, II Tim. 2¹⁸): Christ is the one who did appear and will appear. Christians are assured of 'life' (e.g. I Tim. 1¹⁶; Tit. 1²); but it is mentioned so vaguely that it is impossible to tell whether it signifies life after death or life after the parousia or both (cf. p. 60f.). On this central Pauline subject, our writer is either silent or nebulous.

Similarly, with regard to eschatology in general. A sufficiently vivid sense of the imminent end of the world is undeniably present in these letters (e.g. II Tim. 1¹²; 4⁸). But the references are formalized, and the intense concern with provision for Christian family life and Church structure indicates that the reality of this expectation had faded and other interests had supervened. In practice, the Church was here to stay, for a reasonable time at least, and provision needed to be made. Though on this point comparison can be made with Colossians among the allegedly genuine letters of Paul (cf. p. 78f.), the air we breathe here is that of Luke-Acts and Ephesians, where too the settled position of the Church seems to be presupposed, rather than that of Paul's undoubted works.

Nor does the writer share Paul's sense of Christian existence as being 'in Christ'. He is not without the phrase, but it refers always to Christian qualities (indeed its sense is virtually adjectival, 'Christian'): cf. I Tim. 1¹⁴; 3¹³; II Tim. 1⁹,¹³; 2¹⁰; 3¹². Titus is short, admittedly, but it is still notable that it lacks the expression entirely.

There is no concept of the Church as a close-knit organism, with all freely contributing to the life of the whole. Rather, it is an ordered structure, where each knows his place and has his assigned duties and proper qualities.

In all these areas it is not easy to interpret the evidence in terms of Paul dealing with a different set of topics from those found in his other letters; it is more likely to be a matter of a different writer who has a widely different sense of the structure of Christian faith and life.

This static rather than dynamic sense of the Christian community goes with a narrower and more negative view of the role of law. It is not as in Paul a great principle in the dealings of God with man, with which, for better or worse, all men must reckon; rather it is for the protection of the good (or respectable) (I Tim. 2^{2b}) and the restraint of the wicked – and people can be thought of as falling so simply into these categories. For this writer, who are the wicked? Ah, they are the others (I Tim. 1$^{8ff.}$).

Sometimes, however, our writer reads very much like Paul and uses a few of his chief words. Indeed, throughout his work there are echoes of Paul's works, particularly Romans, as the commentary will illustrate, and it looks as if he may have seen himself as producing an interpretative exegesis of some Pauline texts, in the rabbinic manner. But his standpoint is so strong and so different from Paul's that the echoes are not easily heard; and, as we have seen, unlike the writer of Ephesians he does not generally work by using the actual words of Paul. Where he does, the doctrine is nearly always lost – transposed into a new key, deprived of its cutting edge. The passage just quoted, I Tim. 1^8, with its statement about the goodness of the law, is a striking example of this, when it is compared with Rom. 7^{12} and the agonizing debate in which that is set (cf. p. 53). The same transposition is to be found in Tit. 3^{5,7}, with a statement, as it seems on the face of it, of Paul's doctrine of justification by faith not works (cf. p. 154).

This writer lacks many of the major themes of Paul. What does he put in their place, and where do his interests and ideas come from?

One who gives a swift first reading to these three pieces may well gain the impression that they are hardly concerned with the content of belief at all, and he will be surprised, if he examines our table on p. 19, to see how many passages are placed under the heading of 'doctrine'. Turning to them, he will admittedly discover that the range of subjects – and words – is not very wide; nevertheless he may wonder whether he was misled by his initial sense that these writings were concerned above all with Church order and good behaviour and the avoidance of heresy.

The initial impression may be justified in this respect, that these are indeed the matters which chiefly impelled our writer to set to work. The impulse is protective – in relation to the Church, both with regard to society (I Tim. 2^2; 3^7; Tit. 3$^{1f.}$) and in the face of dissidents (I Tim. 1^{20}; II Tim. 2^{16-18}; Tit. $1^{10f.}$); in relation to Paul's reputation (cf. the glossily moving portrait of Paul in II Timothy); in relation to moral standards (I Tim. $1^{8ff.}$); in relation to Church leaders (I Tim. 4^{12}; and 5^{19}, with its ruling that elders are not to be impugned except in special circumstances); in relation to widows, who are to be entertained as long as they are orthodox, honest and genuine (I Tim. $5^{3ff.}$).

Nevertheless, there is a firm doctrinal base, even if, it may be, circumstances have created a need to attend to matters other than the pure exposition of the faith for its own sake. The doctrinal base is so firm that it is possible to ask whether it has not solidified. That is, has it lost the capacity to inform other areas of Christian reflection? Has it turned into a self-contained body of ideas, which other things rest upon but by which they are not closely affected? The isolated (and forgettable) quality of the doctrinal passages suggests this conclusion. They are almost credal; perhaps some of them (the 'faithful sayings'? p. 59f.) are already hallowed formulas. But this may be going too far if it implies that they are to some degree taken for granted. We must discover what they say.

They find it worthwhile to assert belief in *one God* (I Tim. 2^5) – itself a sign that the writer thinks within the general Hellenistic world and is not bounded intellectually by the presuppositions of Judaism and Christianity (cf. p. 31). God is creator (I Tim. 4^3), but he is also saviour (I Tim. 1^1; 2^3; Tit. 1^3; 3^4) in that he graciously sent Christ (II Tim. 1^9; Tit. 2^{11}), with the result that 'life and immortality' (II Tim. 1^{10}) are now available for those who believe.

Christ is the mediator (I Tim. 1^5). It may be that his heavenly existence before he came into the world is presupposed but it is never referred to explicitly and our writer shows hardly any interest in such speculative concepts. All the emphasis is on his two 'appearings' – in the past and in the future, at the End – for our salvation, indeed for the salvation of all (the expression may or may not be conventional – if the latter, then its problems are not examined, cf. I Tim. 2^4; Tit. 2^{11}). This emphasis too may be owed to the general religious assumptions of the Hellenistic world and show that the writer, perhaps unconsciously, functioned, as a Christian, as part of that wider scene. It is the language of Hellenistic religion, including the emperor cult, which was achieving wider acceptance as the first century came to its close: devotion centred on the longed for manifestation of the deity. The eschatological hope derived from Judaism was capable of some assimilation to this brand of piety and certainly could be expressed in its terminology.

The interpretation of baptism in terms of 'rebirth' in Tit. 3^5 may belong to the same world, linked though it is (cf. also v. 7) with language taken directly from Paul (though not assembled in a Pauline manner). So may the weight put on the title 'saviour' (applied to God and to Christ, cf. p. 47), which appears only once in Paul (Phil. 3^{20}) but no less than ten times in these writings (five times in II Peter). In addition, 'salvation' occurs twice (II Tim. 2^{10}; 3^{15}) and 'save' seven times. (The noun and verb are relatively common also in Paul, but not in the same central role as the general term expressing God's action for man; rather they refer in Paul to the consummation at the Last Day or the process which leads up to it – except in a small minority of passages, e.g. Rom. 8^{24}; II Cor. 6^2.) 'Salvation' was the chief 'benefit' expected of religion in the Hellenistic world at this time, and deities in the mystery cults and other religions of the time were above all 'saviours'. 'God, the saviour' (*theos sōtēr*) was a technical term in this environment.

Our writer finds no difficulty in adopting this language. At the same time, he has no use for the speculation with which it was so often associated (e.g. I Tim. 1^4). Rather it is placed in a context of firm moral teaching – responsible and disciplined godliness. Only once does he approach what we might, in terms of his time, call speculative theology, in the formula in I Tim. 3^{16}. If we, from our present standpoint, are right in scenting here the atmosphere which was to luxuriate into developed Gnosticism, in particular its association with myths concerning descending and ascending divine saviours, then our writer apparently did not find it offensive, perhaps because this example had been too long absorbed into the Church's stock.*

*Gnosticism is often used to denote a number of Christian deviationist sects most of which came into existence in the second century, e.g. the Valentinians and the followers of Basilides. But it is used also (and this is how we use it here) in a more general sense, to signify a religious frame of mind, already discernible in the period when Christianity arose, whose leading features were an intense concern with individual salvation by means of the possession of esoteric saving truth, a depreciation of the material world, and a fondness for

Not that the moral teaching is pure and distinctive Christian material. Most of it is the commonplace ethics of the Hellenistic world of the period.* It would have been shared and applauded by pagans and Jews of many kinds, often influenced by the loosely Stoic ideas widespread at the time as well as by more locally native traditions such as the one derived from Old Testament Law. It was the moral teaching of those who took a more positive view of society in this world than the groups affected by Gnosticism. The interests of the latter seemed to people like our writer to be undisciplined and irresponsible. Hence the provision of both a firm structure of authority (I Tim. 3 and Tit. 1$^{5\mathrm{ff.}}$) and extended exhortation and moral provision for all sections (I Tim. 5; Tit. 2); hence also the determination, so far as in him lies, to encourage the good behaviour of the Church in relation to secular authorities (I Tim. 2$^{1\mathrm{f.}}$; Tit. 3$^{1\mathrm{f.}}$).

What does all this tell us about the authorship of these writings? As far as their lack of Pauline teaching and their way of treating Pauline material are concerned, there remains room for subjective judgement, and some scholars still think that the obvious differences between the other Pauline letters and these writings are not so great that they cannot be accounted for by the passing of years and a change of interest. But this does not reckon with the many signs that we are reading the work of a man who leans upon Paul but has not properly absorbed his teaching, or rather sees it refracted through the prism of his own concerns, and, indeed, has his own almost technical means of treating his source-material, including many passages in Romans. Nor does it most satisfactorily explain the reiterated use in the relatively meagre and segregated doctrinal passages of a small number of ideas, some of them the stereotyped notions of the Hellenistic religious world of the late first century, or the mainly conventional and pedestrian nature of the moral teaching. It is true that Paul is well capable of adapting himself to circumstances and moulding his theological idiom,† but it is scarcely conceivable that he would lose his capacity

---

speculation, often ingenious and bizarre, concerning the universe. It resulted from a wide variety of blends of oriental religion, Greek thought, and, often, Jewish words and ideas.

*cf. R. J. Karris, 'The Background and Significance of the Polemic of the Pastoral Epistles', *JBL*, 92, 1973.

†cf. H. Chadwick, 'All Things to All Men', *NTS*, I, 1955, p. 261ff.

to integrate his theology with his whole subject matter, that he would drop so many of his central ideas, that he would take on so many of the more flatly conventional concepts of the period and use so much of the stock material of Hellenistic Judaism, a source also utilized for such pieces of Old Testament exegesis as the writer incorporates in his work.* Of course, none of this in itself excludes an amanuensis, working largely on his own. For a final decision, we must explore still further.

The personal notes

These passages, which dominate II Timothy, but occupy a smaller place in I Timothy and Titus, have played a crucial role in discussion of the authorship of these letters. For some, they decide the issue without more ado: of course only Paul could have written, or been in some way responsible for, the writings which contain this material. Even if he gave freedom to an amanuensis to write most of the works, for reasons lost to us, perhaps because of urgency, Paul certainly dictated these sections or gave instructions for their inclusion. They could have come from no other source. And for the most part they are so trivial that they could only have been composed alongside the rest.

If this last argument is accepted – and it has much strength – then it confounds another popular account of the make-up of these writings, but it may equally well cohere with a belief in the non-Pauline authorship of these writings as a whole. The other popular view is that the personal notes, or some of them, are fragments of genuine Pauline correspondence incorporated by the devout Paulinist writer in his otherwise pseudonymous works. The fundamental difficulty encountered by such a view is that of implausibility. The notes do not all belong to the same situation in Paul's life, they are brief, and they are, mostly, trivial. How then did they come to be preserved and assembled? These objections help to lead C. F. D. Moule† to reject a 'fragment hypothesis' in favour of a belief in unified authorship by Luke, acting in close association with Paul.

Apart from this difficulty, it is not absolutely clear which passages

---

*e.g. I Tim. 2$^{13-15}$; cf. A. T. Hanson, *Studies in the Pastoral Epistles*, SPCK, 1968.
†'The Problem of the Pastoral Epistles: a Reappraisal', *BJRL*, 47, 1965, p. 448.

ought to be included. Not, surely, all that include personal names, for example the opening greetings: if the letters are not genuine Pauline productions, then these sections are plainly pseudonymous. In his first book (cf. p. 22), Harrison listed five passages which he regarded as genuine Pauline fragments: Tit. 3^{12-15}; II Tim. $4^{13-15,20,}$ ^{21a}; II Tim. 4^{16-18}; II Tim. $4^{9-12,22b}$; II Tim. 1^{16-18}; $3^{10f.}$; $4^{1,2a,5b,6-8,}$ ^{18b,19,21b,22a} (this final letter being, in effect, the basis for the editorial activity out of which the writer produced our II Timothy). In 1964, Harrison stood for three notes only: Tit. 3^{12-15}; II Tim. 4^{9-15}; II Tim. 1^{16-18}; $3^{10f.}$; $4^{1,2a,5b-8,16-19,21b,22a}$. For all of them, he provided possible locations in the story of Paul's life. A. T. Hanson[*] also accepts three fragments: II Tim. 1^{15-18}; 4^{9-21} (omitting v. 18); Tit. 3^{12-14}.

We should note that these theories isolate only those passages which are virtually free of other than personal material. But their being mixed up with other matter is the only factor which excludes such passages as I Tim. 1^{18-20} and II Tim. 2^{17}. Is it really possible to distinguish in this way? Our writer is generally neat in the arranging of his material: we did not find it very difficult to make the analysis on p. 19. But just as occasionally a few words of doctrinal material appear in a passage mainly devoted to another topic (e.g. I Tim. 1^{15}), so sometimes personal notes are incorporated into sections concerned with heresy, while for the most part they are kept separate in their own compartments.

Another difficulty lies within the most substantial note itself. Harrison, with reason, saw II Tim. 4 as containing parts of more than one Pauline note. If vv. 6–21 are taken as a whole, then it is indeed hard to see why a Paul who was on the verge of execution (v. 6) should ask for his cloak and books (v. 13). On almost any view, this collocation is a problem, but it is not at all impossible if the writer's chief interest was not that of either using or contributing to the life-story of Paul.

So we turn to the possibility that this material is fictitious. The crux of the matter is II Timothy, where, as Harrison's analysis allowed, the personal material dominates the scene. We have already given a way of looking at the three writings together which may account for this (p. 19f.), as well as for the comparative dearth of such material in I Timothy and, to a lesser degree, Titus.

[*] op. cit., p. 135, n. 11.

INTRODUCTION

Then should we not judge the personal notes simply as part of a total scenario, of which 'Timothy' and 'Titus' themselves are the most important elements? From this point of view, I Timothy is in fact as 'personal' as the other writings, though not in the same way: it concentrates on the figure of 'Timothy' (4^{12-15}; $6^{11ff.}$, where he is enjoined to behave as 'Paul' will at his end, cf. II Tim. 4^7), and, to a lesser degree, on 'Paul' ($1^{13ff.}$). All is equally fictitious. The writer draws upon the Pauline epistles (especially Rom. 16), perhaps upon Acts, perhaps upon other stories about Paul and his entourage; he may even have invented some of the names – the legendary Acts of Paul and other similar writings in profusion were not far away.* His concern is partly to provide verisimilitude – Pauline realism – just as the greetings make possible the letter format. It is partly also to paint Paul, the 'authority figure', as not only an impressive but also an inspiring and moving example from an already heroic past (cf. Acts). This is done chiefly in II Timothy.

It is vital for our writer that, in an uncertain present, when heresy was hard to grapple with and when it was not easy to find criteria on which to base oneself, there should be a past to appeal to. Nevertheless, his eye is mainly on the present: in 'Timothy' and 'Titus' we can see the leaders of congregations in the writer's own day, with a history of Church organization and disputing behind them; in Hymenaeus, Alexander and the like, the troublesome heretics; in Onesiphorus the admirable, faithful and orthodox Christians of his time. So the incongruities in the more personal passages lose their force; as do the problems of 'fitting in' some of these details with other evidence concerning Paul's career (cf. p. 135) – this was not one of our writer's goals. We have no need to struggle with the data to find a niche for a Pauline mission in Crete (Tit. 1^5); or to reconcile the implication of I Clement 5† and, as far as it goes, of Acts that Paul suffered only one Roman imprisonment before his martyrdom, with the necessary assumption from II Timothy 4, if the details are taken as historical, that Paul suffered a second imprisonment there (1^{17}) before his death (cf. 4^{16} with its reference to a former trial). Nor do we need, alternatively, to reconcile one possible implication of I Clement 5, that Paul made a journey to Spain after a first Roman imprisonment (for when else did he go there?), with a possible impli-

*cf. Hennecke, II, p. 322ff.   †ECW, p. 25.

cation of I Timothy 1[3] that he visited Ephesus in this period. No need either, if we insist, on stylistic grounds, that I and II Timothy were written close together, to hold to a gap between the two imprisonments during which Paul had time to visit Ephesus (I Tim. 1[3]) and (was he now in prison again, with his execution still not decided?) even hoped to do so again (3[14]); or, if identity of situation for the two letters is thought impossible, to explain how such similar writings can have come from different parts of Paul's career.

Nor is it to the point to complain* of the 'gratuitous irony and bad taste' in writing of coming visits by Paul and Timothy (I Tim. 3[14ff.]; 4[13]) long after Paul has died. These details, imitated from the Corinthians letters, are simply part of the total apparatus.

We must now turn to the questions: what made such behaviour on the part of this writer both possible and desirable? What circumstances made him write thus in Paul's name?

PURPOSE

Continuity in religious devotion, both at its profounder levels and in the way of rituals, is possible in certain respects and perhaps more desirable than either our society or most of our present-day Churches often appreciate.† But continuous identity in religious thought, whether desirable or not, is a chimera, no less so for being much sought and greatly cherished. A theological tradition may determine consciously to preserve itself unchanged and intact over the years; but general thought and cultural forms shift around it. Without realizing it, its own defenders look at it through different eyes from their predecessors, utter old words with changed emphasis and sense. It is not only that the perspectives of thought have changed. New pressures have arisen to which men are compelled to react. New problems are to be solved, new controversies engaged in. And while conservative instinct prompts recourse to familiar tools and weapons,

*C. F. D. Moule, 'The Problem of the Pastoral Epistles: a Reappraisal', *BJRL*, 47, 1965, p. 447.

†cf. Mary Douglas, *Natural Symbols*, Penguin, 1973.

they are, intuitively if not deliberately, remoulded for the perform-
ance of fresh tasks.

So it has been throughout the history of the Christian Church; so
it already was in the last years of the first century and the first decades
of the second. Our evidence is meagre and fragmentary, and we must
beware of generalizing for the Church as a whole. But in some parts
of the Church at least, some earlier controversies had faded. For example, the question whether Christians (Gentile or Jewish) were
really a brand of Jews and Christianity a Jewish sect, bound to retain
adequate marks of Jewishness, however defined, had been largely
settled in favour of the Church's independence. The first decisive
steps towards this had come from the powerful influence of Paul,
who saw the religious question in a radically new light, by which
Jew and Gentile were on the same footing. This resulted from the
liberating influence of ideas which led him to see the key to men's
relationship with God in Jesus the redeemer rather than in observance
of the Law – ideas which belonged in a general way to the Gnostic
world of thought (cf. p. 30), but arose for Paul from his own
tumultuous religious experience.

Events had provided decisive support for this aspect of Paul's
theology. The fall of Jerusalem in A.D. 70 has left hardly a trace in the
documents which make up the New Testament (cf. Matt. 22[7]; Luke
21[20]), but it must have been crucial for the fortunes of the Christian
Church, which was in any case becoming increasingly weighted towards the Gentile world and increasingly Gentile in composition. In
the crisis of the Jewish revolt of A.D. 66–70, the evidence (admittedly
meagre) is that Christians declined to join in the national struggle
(Mark 13[9f.]) and that the breach between them and the main stream
of Judaism in Palestine became irreparable (cf. the excommunication
referred to in John 16[2], dating from about A.D. 85).

More important, the Christian congregation in Jerusalem, hitherto
the 'mother church' of the entire Christian body, as we may suppose,
removed itself to Pella, and by departing from the sacred site seems
to have condemned itself to oblivion. The Church was now without
a headquarters, without any semblance of central leadership, even
disputed leadership, without clear criteria for policy, theology or
development. And not long afterwards came the emergence into
something like concrete form of the first fundamental doctrinal dis-

sension in the Christian body; the beginnings of Gnosticism (cf. p. 30).* Essentially this showed itself, at this stage, in a weakening of a sense of history and divine providence in the world, and in a central emphasis on Jesus as a purely heavenly saviour who came temporarily to earth.

As we have suggested, Paul himself was sufficiently affected by this kind of thought for it to have helped to lead him to his sense of the newness, independence and distinctiveness of the faith centred on Jesus and of the Church which proclaimed it. To this degree, it had already been decisive in the development of Christianity.

To trace the steps by which Christian theological reflection moved in the decades after Paul's death is a task fraught with uncertainty. Examples of Christian thought in this period are available to us among the books of the New Testament and elsewhere, but the inner story of the theological development is obscure, and we can be sure that it differed from one part of the Church to another. What follows is therefore one tentative account of an uncertain phase in Christian doctrinal history, with one product of which this book is concerned.

As far as the Gnostic style of thought was concerned, it seems that whereas in Paul its contribution was to help turn the shape of his thought away from the heritage of Judaism and the Law to Jesus as the divinely sent saviour, it soon expressed itself among some Christians much more diffusely and by way of its more general characteristics. So in those Christian circles which were influenced by it, we find the emergence of exuberant speculation about the heavenly world, a fondness for esoteric religiosity, and a tendency to depreciate the material and bodily aspects of life in this world.

At much the same time as these tendencies were beginning to make headway among some Christians, the Gospels, giving their accounts of the life, death, and resurrection of Jesus, were being written. It may be that one factor in their emergence was a feeling that concentration upon Jesus was being eroded by these more speculative Christians. Those groups which produced the Gospels clearly saw the centrality of Jesus as essential to the very being of Christianity, now distinct from its Jewish parent-body. For them, the Church's main stream,

---

*See S. G. F. Brandon, *The Fall of Jerusalem and the Christian Church*, SPCK, 1951, for one view of this crisis.

Jesus became more and more vital, not just from the point of view of devotion to him but in the structure of belief.

While for some the centrality of Jesus thus expressed itself through attention to accounts of his words and deeds, it may well be the case that others preferred to put it in more formal doctrinal terms. There are signs that this was so among those who wrote the Pastoral Epistles. In them, Jesus appears as a rather static figure within theological formulas (e.g. II Tim. $1^{9f.}$; Tit. 3^{4-7}). He has neither the personal vividness found in the Gospels nor is he the object of quite that intensity of feeling, as an intimately discerned saviour, which we find in Paul. 'Man' he may be (I Tim. 2^5), but even in II Timothy, with its strongly personal atmosphere, there is none of the close identity with Christ found in a passage like Gal. 2^{20}. Rather, he is a somewhat formal figure, with certain definite roles – to appear, to judge, and to inspire. Even in the particularly moving passage, II Tim. 4^{6-8}, he is 'the Lord', 'the righteous judge'. It may be of course that the different genre of writing sufficiently explains this feature; but the facts remain that this genre has been selected and the formulas have been produced, as a matter of deliberate choice at a time when fluidity of choice was available.

This formalization at the christological level meant that there was a need to find flexibility elsewhere. It coincided with another urgent necessity: to find criteria for right belief, authorities you could trust and reasons for them. Paul had already found that all sorts of people in all sorts of causes could appeal to the name 'Christ' (II Cor. 11^4; cf. Matt. $7^{21ff.}$). It appears that, at a lower level, they could also appeal to the name 'Paul'. And here there was more room for manoeuvre. In the first place, he was not the subject of formal doctrinal statements, neither defined nor restricted by them. In the second place, many Christians (and among them those in what were becoming the more influential areas, especially Asia Minor) had access to his writings. Nobody had such rich and direct sources for Jesus.

In the third place, Paul's mind had been ingenious, brilliant and many-sided. In Christian theology, he had been the pioneer. He had explored new ways of speech and left them still malleable. He had tried first this idiom, then that, so that later, more prosaically minded men could take him in more than one way. All the more so, when the issues which had led him to formulate his teaching had, many of them, passed by, and he was therefore read in the light of different situations – and pressed into service as a determining voice in disputes which had never, in their new forms at least, crossed his mind. There is a sense then that controversy which might have centred on the figure of Jesus came to centre in this period on Paul instead, and he became the hero of rival interests. Sometimes he was ignored altogether because of the associations his name had acquired.*

Paul's sharply independent attitude to at least some elements in the Jerusalem Church, albeit within an acceptance of that institution's authority (cf. Gal. 1–2), led some, in the period after its removal, to take Paul as the apostle of the Church's opposition to all things Jewish. His teaching about the Law, in fact complex, agonized, and belonging very much to his own situation, was taken as grist to the same mill. The name chiefly associated with this view of Paul was Marcion, whose influence in the Christian world of the mid second century can scarcely be exaggerated.

Others were led to seize upon not only Paul's apparent antiJewishness and antinomianism (what a one-sided reading of him it was!) but also his flights in a speculative direction, with Christ as a heavenly redeemer figure exalted among the cosmic hierarchy (cf. Phil. 2^{6-11}; Col. 1^{15-20}). This vein, modest enough by later Gnostic standards, was nevertheless capable of exploitation; and, like the Gospel of John, Paul became a valued authority for many of the Gnostics.

But he was too important a figure in the Christian treasury to be ceded without a struggle. Some second-century writers, for whom much of his teaching was in itself congenial, chose to ignore his work, as they chose to ignore the Gospel of John – presumably because both were tainted and suspect. This appears to be true of Hegesippus, Papias (about both of whom our information is limited and mostly indirect, through the fourth-century historian, Eusebius), and Justin. What alarmed them above all was the suspicion of antinomianism. For them, Christianity was clearly a moral guide, whatever else it was besides. Gnostics were notoriously weak in this regard, and Paul could too easily be enlisted in support.

*See C. K. Barrett, 'Pauline Controversies in the Early Church', *NTS*, 20, 1974, pp. 229–45; M. F. Wiles, *The Divine Apostle*, Cambridge University Press, 1967.

The writer of the Pastoral Epistles was less easily deterred. He grasped the nettle, and gave us a clear-cut 'anti-antinomian' Paul (cf. I Tim. 1^8, alluding to a text in Paul himself, in Romans (7^{12}) no less; also the extensive moral teaching throughout). The author of Acts moved along a different but parallel, and sometimes converging, path, showing that Paul, far from being reluctant to accept the constituted authorities of the Church, was at every turn an obedient son, who constantly subordinated himself to the leaders in Jerusalem.* That is, Paul was by no means suitable to be the darling of deviationists. In Acts $20^{29ff.}$, in the course of a speech, which like II Tim. $4^{6ff.}$ has the quality of a final testament (it is Paul's only speech in Acts to a Christian audience), he himself foresees these evils which will arise. Clearly, it is a matter which deeply moves the writer and one on which he is keen to enlist the full sympathy of his readers (cf. especially vv. 29f.). On this issue, Acts and the Pastoral Epistles come together (cf. I Tim. $1^{4ff.}$, etc.). Paul is not the proto-Gnostic, but the anti-Gnostic. And for Acts too, Paul took a more positive view of the Law than the Paul of history was alleged to have done, cf. 15^{20}; 21^{26}.

That the Pastoral Epistles arose as an element in the struggle for the inheritance of Paul is supported by some early evidence concerning the content of collections of the Pauline epistles. Marcion himself appears not to have known, or at any rate accepted, the Pastorals; and an important third-century manuscript of the Pauline epistles (P46), the oldest extant, probably did not contain them.† Marcion may have had reason deliberately to leave aside these writings (though if they had already been part and parcel of the Pauline collection, II Timothy, so strongly pro-Paul, at least might have appealed to him and none of the three would have been impossible for him to adapt to his purposes); and it is conceivable that they were written partly to oppose him (see below, p. 102). As far as it goes, then, this evidence points to a date for these writings in the first half of the second century, certainly some decades after Paul's death and probably after the collection of the main body of the Pauline writings. It therefore confirms the conclusions reached in our considerations of

* cf. E. Haenchen, *The Acts of the Apostles*, Blackwell, 1971, pp. 110–16; W. Schmithals, *Paul and James*, SCM, 1963.
† cf. B. M. Metzger, *The Text of the New Testament*, Oxford University Press, 1964, p. 37f.

INTRODUCTION

'Authorship'. And if we have at all correctly identified the context of Christian life and thought in which they originated, with its conflicts and anxieties, and if the Pastorals at all 'ring true' in that context, then theories concerning the use of an amanuensis are as wide of the mark as belief in Pauline authorship; and hypotheses concerning genuine Pauline fragments lose force.

What then is to be said positively about the provenance of these works?

As we have seen, their links in the New Testament are with Acts and (cf. p. 27) Ephesians. Together they make up the canonized testimony to the early development of what came to be regarded as 'orthodox' Paulinism. In Rome at least, the Pastoral Epistles had achieved that position by the end of the second century: the Muratorian Canon lists them straightforwardly with the rest of the Pauline writings and in the same sentence as the Letter to Philemon (i.e. putting together letters addressed to individuals rather than churches).* Shortly before, Irenaeus of Lyons opened his great work, *Against Heresies*, suitably with an allusion to I Tim. 1⁴. From that time on, their place as Pauline epistles within the canon of Scripture was assured.

Earlier, their story is more problematic. There are numerous points of comparison between the Pastorals and the Christian writers of the late first and early second centuries, in particular I Clement and Ignatius.† These verbal links are listed by Spicq.‡ None of them amounts to an indication of quotation – in either direction. They speak rather for life in the same world and period (cf. Harrison's use of them, p. 22f.). We cannot discount this absence of quotation in the case of either Clement or Ignatius by saying that they would have been unwilling, like some orthodox writers of a few decades later, to use Paul because he had become the hero of heretical groups (cf. p. 102). Ignatius is happy to quote I Corinthians, and I Clement reveres Paul. We cannot tell whether this absence of reference to the Pastorals is attributable to their not being linked with his works in common circulation, or to their not being in existence.

A novel and somewhat surprising possibility needs to be mentioned at this point. Among the haul of Dead Sea Scrolls from Cave 7, a

* cf. J. Stevenson, *A New Eusebius*, SPCK, 1957, p. 146.   † cf. *ECW*.
‡ Commentary, I, p. 162ff.

41

number have been identified by J. O'Callaghan as possibly containing pieces of the Gospel of Mark and other New Testament books. Among them is one which he has reconstructed as I Tim. 3^{16} and $4^{1,3}$. The hand is dated to the late first or early second century. However, only seventeen letters are decipherable and other reconstructions are possible, yielding Old Testament passages.*

The earliest clear reference to them is by way of an isolated, unacknowledged quotation in the *Letter to the Philippians* (ch. 4) by Polycarp, Bishop of Smyrna, writing perhaps in the late thirties of the second century. He reproduces I Tim. 6^{10} and 6^7. In ch. 9 of his letter, there is another phrase in common with our writings. Speaking of Paul and other martyrs and saints, he says that 'they did not love the present world', using the same wording as II Tim. 4^{10}.

This verbal link, together with numerous other features of situation and interest led H. von Campenhausen to suggest that Polycarp himself might have been the author of the Pastoral Epistles.† Both are 'ecclesiastical' in their interest and firmly anti-Gnostic. Polycarp certainly and the Pastorals plausibly belong to Asia Minor. Unlike a number of his contemporaries who belonged to the 'orthodox' camp, Polycarp was not afraid of appealing to the name of Paul – our writer shared his enthusiasm.‡ He also quoted Paul several times. He had as his scribe or messenger one Crescens, cf. II Tim. 4^{10}. He used four words which, in the New Testament, are found only in the Pastorals (Greek *mataiologia*, vain discussion; *egkratēs*, self-controlled; *diabolos* (as adjective), slanderous; *dilogos*, double-tongued). Only these two writers, apart from Ignatius in a brief reference in his Letter to Polycarp, 4, deal with the question of the conduct of Christian widows (I Tim. 5 and Polycarp, Phil. 4). Both writings seem to have a similar view of the status and role of the Christian leader in his congregation.

All these features, drawn out persuasively by von Campenhausen, do not add up to a proof of identity of authorship. But they certainly

---

*cf. A. C. Urban, *Revue de Qumran*, 8, 1973; see also J. O'Callaghan, *Biblica*, 53, 1972; and P. Benoit, *Revue biblique*, 80, 1973, with photographs of the texts in question; he rejects O'Callaghan's reconstruction. Clearly no firm trust can be placed in this evidence.

†See 'Polykarp von Smyrna und die Pastoralbriefe', *Sitzungsberichte der heidelberger Akademie der Wissenschaften*, Heidelberg, 1951.

‡cf. Polycarp, Phil., Chs. 3, 9, 11, *ECW*, p. 144ff.

confirm the rightness of placing our writings in the first half of the second century – and later rather than earlier.

It remains to identify more closely the enemies against whom these writings direct their thrust. On the basis of a possible cryptic reference to Marcion's book, *The Contradictions*, in I Tim. 6^{20}, it has sometimes been suggested that the enemy was the teaching of that powerful heresiarch. But the idea is generally rejected because our writer shares Marcion's anti-Jewish tendency, cf. Tit. 1^{14}. The association with Polycarp, however, forces us to take the suggestion seriously, for he was the bitter enemy of Marcion.

We may suppose that the attack in these writings has several prongs. It is directed against deviationists of all kinds.* While disputes about the law are mentioned in I Tim. 1^7, Jewish enemies are referred to explicitly only in Tit. $1^{10ff.}$ – and then they soon seem to merge rather surprisingly into Cretans. In fact, it is far from obvious that there is much reality in the Jewish quality of these heretics. This is not their dominant characteristic, and the reference may even be a piece of Pauline stage-setting (cf. the use of the Pauline term, 'the circumcision party', in v. 10). Even if the heretics, or some of them, really were Jewish, the attack is wider: it is on Gnostic tendencies in general, and Marcion, or men of like mind, would easily come under that condemnation, with their depreciation of the creator God (cf. I Tim. 4^4).

Our writer would not have approved of Marcion's rejection of the Old Testament: see II Tim. $3^{15f.}$, with its firm teaching. He was sufficiently skilled in its exegesis to engage in a small but significant number of exercises in that field (cf. p. 71f.).

Indeed, though his own milieu is firmly that of the Christian Church, now independent of Judaism, so that he looks back on the Jewish heritage with no sense of conflict, he owes much of his for-

*J. M. Ford, 'Proto-Montanism in the Pastoral Epistles', *NTS*, 17, 1971, pp. 338–46, suggests that the heretics were possibly an early manifestation of a brand of heresy which shortly afterwards broke out in earnest under the leadership of Montanus of Phrygia. That powerful movement was prophetic and charismatic in character – hence the Pastoral's stress on sobriety. It gave a prominent place to women so threatening the place of the regular ministry – hence our writer's care to regulate their role in the congregation (I Tim. $2^{8ff.}$; 5) and to define the authority of overseer, elders and deacons (I Tim. 3; Tit. $1^{5ff.}$).

mation to Hellenistic Judaism (cf. p. 71). He is, in fact, a man of the Hellenistic world, perhaps Asia Minor, able to draw upon the varied intellectual resources of the time. While he is wholly committed to his Christianity, there is a sense in which he is, like the author of Acts, a man who belongs to a pluralist society, upon which he looks out with interest, tolerance and some satisfaction. He is not disinclined to share its better moral teaching or over-determined to integrate it (like Paul) with Christian doctrine.

Such is the man who, for the sake of Christ and the faith, endeavours to safeguard the heritage of Paul for his own times, and to portray an ideal which has a practical nobility not to be despised.

FURTHER READING

Commentaries are best classified according to their attitude to the question of authorship.

In favour of Pauline authorship (using an amauensis), recent works include:

J. N. D. Kelly, *The Pastoral Epistles*, New Testament Commentaries, A. & C. Black, 1963.

C. Spicq, *Études bibliques*, 4th ed., 2 vols., 1969.

J. Jeremias, *Das Neue Testament Deutsch*, 1953.

Against Pauline authorship:

C. K. Barrett, *The Pastoral Epistles*, Oxford University Press, 1963.

Dibelius/Conzelmann, *Handbuch zum Neuentestament*, English translation in Hermeneia Series, Fortress Press, 1972.

Other literature is referred to at the appropriate point in the Introduction and Commentary. Perhaps the most useful general orientation is provided by H. von Campenhausen, *Ecclesiastical Authority and Spiritual Power in the Church of the First Three Centuries*, A. & C. Black, 1969.

To these works the present commentary is indebted.

The First Letter to Timothy

THE OPENING GREETING

1 Paul, an apostle of Christ Jesus by command of God our Saviour and of Christ Jesus our hope, 2 to Timothy, my true child in the faith: grace, mercy, and peace from God the Father and Christ Jesus our Lord.

In general form, the opening greeting is typical of letters of the period. The form is: A to B, greeting.* In this, our letter is like the undoubted letters of Paul. It resembles those letters also in the way the usual bare greeting is elaborated. Paul used the greetings at the head of his letters to make highly significant theological points. His imitator and follower adopts the same practice, though perhaps in a more formal spirit.

Most elements in these verses have parallels in the genuine letters. There are however one or two special features which merit attention. Most of Paul's letters bear the greetings not only of Paul himself but also of his associates. The exceptions are Romans, Galatians – and Ephesians. The first case may be explained by the generally less personal nature of the work: it is probably written to a congregation of which Paul has little intimate knowledge, certainly one with which he has had no direct contact.† In the second case, paradoxically as it may appear, it may be that the impetuously personal manner in which Paul begins the letter may have made him ignore any friends who were with him (at least there was an amanuensis, cf. Gal. 6^{11}). Perhaps Ephesians gives us a closer parallel. Here too Pauline authorship is doubted, on many varied grounds.‡ Here too we suspect the presence of a Pauline admirer and disciple. Here too Paul is understandably placed on a pedestal. He is a venerated figure. To associate others with him would detract from the very point which the writer wishes to make. Those who argue for Pauline authorship will natur-

*For examples, see G. Milligan, *Greek Papyri*, Cambridge University Press, 1910.
† See however, Paul S. Minear, *The Obedience of Faith*, SCM, 1971.
‡ See J. L. Houlden, *Paul's Letters from Prison*, Penguin, 1970, p. 241ff.

ally retort that the truth is simply that Paul was alone at the time of writing. They must then account for the opening of II Timothy, which again comes from Paul alone, though Luke is with him (II Tim. 4[11]). It is more likely that here, as in Ephesians, we are witnessing the beginning of the process whereby Paul is, at least for the Christians who sponsored these writings, the revered hero of the recent past, the anchor of true doctrine.

This view is strengthened by another special feature of the greeting which heads this letter (as also the other Pastoral Epistles). Unlike all the extant genuine letters, these letters are addressed to individuals rather than congregations (Philemon, though it mentions names, is really no exception). There is nothing remarkable in that in itself. But Timothy, who appears elsewhere as Paul's colleague (*fellow-worker* – there is no reason to undervalue the term – in Rom. 16[21]; cf. II Cor. 1[1]; Phil. 1[1]; etc.), appears here as *my true child*. Even if he was Paul's convert – and the story about Timothy in Acts 16[1-3] does not refer to the point – there is no doubt that he is portrayed in these letters in a much more firmly subordinate position than in the genuine letters. Paul is the master and the senior, Timothy (and Titus, cf. Tit. 1[4], and no doubt those church officers of Pauline congregations whom they represent) is the pupil and the junior. This portrayal has considerable bearing on the questions of date and authorship, cf. pp. 34, 40.

If this interpretation is correct, it affects the understanding of the title *apostle* accorded to Paul. Originally signifying missionary or emissary and representative (see especially Gal. 1 for a vivid picture of what it meant for Paul, cf. I Cor. 9[1ff.]), it seems that towards the end of the first century it came in Christian usage to carry overtones of 'founding father' or 'authoritative leader'. Understandably, these connotations came to be attached to the great figures of the Church's early days, as the Christians of the next generations looked back to them. While in Paul himself the word is applied to a number of figures (cf. Rom. 16[7]; Phil. 2[25]; I Cor. 15[7]; Gal. 1[19]) and with varying degrees of technicality, later Christian usage seems to have narrowed it down more firmly. For the writer of Acts, apart from two references in ch. 14 (where it is applied to Paul and Barnabas, vv. 4 and 14), it is reserved for the Twelve (including Matthias, the substitute for Judas), and the concept of 'the Twelve Apostles' is clearly established: in the eyes of this writer, they were the authoritative governing body of the Church in its first years. It is a picture which does great violence to the consciousness of the historical Paul that he was indubitably an apostle, on a par with the rest (I Cor. 9^1; 15$^{3\text{ff.}}$). The writer of Acts also gives honour and great prominence to Paul, while at the same time maintaining his picture of the Twelve as the Church's rulers and the agents of continuity with the lifetime of Jesus (Acts 1$^{21-6}$). The writers of Ephesians and the Pastoral Epistles have no interest in accommodating the Twelve: for them Paul is the figure whose aegis assures authority and security, and *apostle* conveys that sense. The word has no article with it: it is simply *apostle* or (perhaps less accurately, with RSV) 'an apostle'. There were soon to be Christians, like Marcion, admittedly a deviant from the main paths of belief, who could refer to Paul as '*the* apostle', a unique figure.

1

Christ Jesus: This order is used in the opening verse of Romans, I and II Corinthians, Philippians, Colossians, and Ephesians. It is unlikely that, here at any rate, there is any special force in the placing of what is strictly a title (*Christ* = Messiah) before the name, Jesus. By this time, the two words, in either order, had become simply a double name, especially in Gentile Christian circles.

by command of God: this is the same point as we find in Gal. 1^1, but here it is made calmly not polemically. The apostle's authority is of divine not human provenance. The formula (as it surely is here) recurs in Tit. 1^3.

our Saviour: the word (*sōtēr*) is much less common in the New Testament than common Christian usage might lead one to suppose. The only use of it in Paul's undoubted letters refers to Jesus (Phil. 3^{20}). The same is true of Eph. 5^{23}. It occurs no less than ten times in the Pastoral Epistles (out of twenty-four occurrences in the whole New Testament). Six times (including the present case and the other two uses in I Timothy, 2^3 and 4^{10}) it refers to God, and four times to Jesus. Titus has three references to each. In genuine Paul, the cognate words ('save' and 'salvation') refer usually to the completion of God's work on the Last Day, either directly or in so far as present life looks forward to that consummation (e.g. Phil. 3^{20}; I Cor. 1^{18}). Except in Tit. 2^{13}, no such reference is in mind in these writings, and it is positively excluded by a passage like Tit. 3⁴. For what it is worth, this tells against the Pauline authorship of these writings.

The word was common in pagan circles for gods and emperors; but it is also common in the LXX as a designation for God, e.g. Ps. 25 (LXX 24)⁵; Is. 12²; 17¹⁰, as well as for heroes like the judges, cf. Jud. 3⁹. Whether the application of the term in our writings to God (and indeed to Jesus as the bringer of salvation) owes more to the LXX, perhaps together with the piety of Hellenistic Judaism, or to the cult of rulers and the mystery religions so popular at the time, it is hard to say. The Pastoral Epistles have little clear reference to Old Testament passages; on the other hand they are far from redolent of the heady and speculative religiosity of the pagan cults, though a word like *epiphaneia* (appearing) in II Tim. 1¹⁰ (cf. also Tit. 3⁴) also belongs to their vocabulary.

Whatever its origin in Christian usage, whether applied to God or to Jesus, it seems not to have become at all fashionable until late in the first century. Not until then do we find the distinct formula 'God our saviour' (cf. Jude 25 as well as the passages in our writings; Lk. 1⁴⁷ is much more obviously septuagintal). As a formal title for Jesus also it grows in popularity at the same period (cf. II Peter 1¹; 2²⁰). Ignatius of Antioch in particular made fairly frequent use of it, e.g. Eph. 1¹; Philad. 9² (*ECW*, pp. 75 and 114), in ways not unlike the writer of the Pastorals. It was in general a most serviceable title for conveying, in not too concrete a manner, a 'high' view of Christ, certainly tending towards the divine.

our hope: in Col. 1²⁷, Paul has a comparable use of this word as a predicate for Christ. Ignatius also has it: Eph. 21² ('Jesus Christ our common hope'); Magn. 11; Philad. 11². The Christian hope centred concretely on Jesus, in particular on his expected return.

true child in the faith: true (*gnēsios*) ordinarily means 'legitimate'. Here the phrase witnesses to Timothy as the authentic follower of Paul, a trustworthy bearer of his inheritance. The image appears in Paul with reference to converts in general rather than Christian leaders, cf. I Cor. 4¹⁵. The transfer of application is in line with the interests of our writer and the concerns of the period in which he writes. *In the faith:* the article is absent but should probably be supplied in the light of a common sense of the word in these writings, signifying, virtually, 'the Christian religion'.

2

grace, mercy, and peace: For this three-part formula, cf. in the New
Testament only II Tim. I² and II John³. The writer has brought together words of greeting and blessing which in genuine Paul (and indeed in Jewish usage) are found singly and in pairs. *Charis* (here, grace)
is also the ordinary word at the head of Hellenistic letters, meaning
'greeting'. In Paul, 'grace' and 'peace' appear together in, for example,
I Cor. I³ and II Cor. I². 'Mercy' and 'peace' combine in Gal. 6¹⁶, and
in II Baruch 78².★ All three are rich Old Testament terms: *grace* and
mercy refer to the rich loving-kindness of God, and *peace* is the leading
characteristic of wholly satisfactory life under him. Here, however, they
have begun to find their way, by means of Paul, into ordinary Christian
usage in the Hellenistic world where these full-blooded associations are
somewhat weakened.

our Lord: one of the earliest titles for Jesus, dating at least from the early
days of the Aramaic-speaking churches; cf. the word *Maranatha*, I Cor.
16²², 'Our Lord, come'. It carried over easily into the Hellenistic
world, for there too it was a title commonly applied to deities and
venerated persons. So it was a natural word to express the devotion
and awe of some of the earliest Greek Christians, cf. I Cor. 12³. And
as the word used in the LXX to translate the divine name Yahweh, it
facilitated the application to Jesus of Old Testament texts which originally referred to God himself. In this way it was crucial in the process of
doctrinal development, cf. e.g. Rom. 10⁹⁻¹³.

I³⁻²⁰   TIMOTHY'S TASK

3 *As I urged you when I was going to Macedonia, remain at Ephesus
that you may charge certain persons not to teach any different doctrine,* 4 *nor
to occupy themselves with myths and endless genealogies which promote
speculations rather than the divine training*ᵃ *that is in faith;* 5 *whereas the
aim of our charge is love that issues from a pure heart and a good conscience
and sincere faith.* 6 *Certain persons by swerving from these have wandered
away into vain discussion,* 7 *desiring to be teachers of the law, without understanding either what they are saying or the things about which they make
assertions.*

★cf. Charles, II, p. 521.

8 *Now we know that the law is good, if any one uses it lawfully,* 9 *under-standing this, that the law is not laid down for the just but for the lawless and disobedient, for the ungodly and sinners, for the unholy and profane, for murderers of mothers, for manslayers,* 10 *immoral persons, sodomites, kid-nappers, liars, perjurers, and whatever else is contrary to sound doctrine,* 11 *in accordance with the glorious gospel of the blessed God with which I have been entrusted.*

12 *I thank him who has given me strength for this, Christ Jesus our Lord, because he judged me faithful by appointing me to his service,* 13 *though I formerly blasphemed and persecuted and insulted him; but I received mercy because I had acted ignorantly in unbelief,* 14 *and the grace of our Lord overflowed for me with the faith and love that are in Christ Jesus.* 15 *The saying is sure and worthy of full acceptance, that Christ Jesus came into the world to save sinners;* 16 *but I received mercy for this reason, that in me, as the foremost, Jesus Christ might display his perfect patience for an example to those who were to believe in him for eternal life.* 17 *To the King of ages, immortal, invisible, the only God, be honour and glory for ever and ever.*[b] *Amen.*

18 *This charge I commit to you, Timothy, my son, in accordance with the prophetic utterances which pointed to you, that inspired by them you may wage the good warfare,* 19 *holding faith and a good conscience. By rejecting conscience, certain persons have made shipwreck of their faith,* 20 *among them Hymenaeus and Alexander, whom I have delivered to Satan that they may learn not to blaspheme.*

[a]Or *stewardship*, or *order*   [b]Greek *to the ages of ages*

In formal letters of our period, especially on a religious subject, it was customary to follow the greeting with thanksgiving to the gods. Paul follows this Hellenistic practice in all his letters apart from Galatians, though in II Corinthians (as in Ephesians) the pattern is modified in accordance with Jewish liturgical practice.* In Titus this element is omitted altogether; in II Timothy it appears in the ex-pected place; here it is delayed to v. 12.

Any attempt to explain these phenomena is bound to be tentative. If our writings were authentic Pauline letters, then they would cer-tainly be difficult to account for. But assuming them to be a set of

*See Paul Schubert, *The Form and Function of the Pauline Thanksgivings*, ZNTW, Beiheft, XX, Berlin, 1939.

pseudonymous writings which are not strictly letters at all, we may attempt to penetrate the writer's intentions. In Titus, as the third of the set, he is keen to come straight to the meat of his message. The difficulty then remains that if the three works were designed as a group, it is hard to see why Titus, containing so little significant fresh material, was written at all, except perhaps to give an impression of the geographical range of Paul's or the writer's concern (or for a reason suggested in p. 19f.). In II Timothy, the most personal of the three works and coming in the middle, when the main positions have been established, the writer finds it natural to follow the customary form.

In our present case, it was, so it seems, more important to make certain preliminary points than to follow slavishly Paul's epistolary habits. If this is correct, then these points give us a guide to the writer's priorities. Two things needed to be done urgently, as soon as he took up his pen. First, he must give an impression of Pauline authenticity by means of geographical reference (v. 3). Second, and more important, he must give an unmistakable account of the doctrinal and moral evils to whose destruction he is dedicated. These matters occupy the forefront of his mind. They form the urgent threat to which he responds. Their prominence is an indication of that urgency.

It is equally important that the eradication of the evils should be authorized by Paul. So the statement of them leads straight into what is obviously intended to be another 'authentically' Pauline passage, only this time it is not geographical but theological-cum-autobiographical. To this purpose the writer devotes his thanksgiving section (vv. 12–17).

But what an odd note it sounds! It is like a piece of music in the style of a great composer, which imitates his conventions, but consistently skims off their brilliance and mistakes their significance. This is one of the most Pauline passages in the Pastorals: it is to stamp the writing as from the master's hand. So there is much about faith and about the apostle's conversion. Yet consistently the expression is not quite true to Paul and just fails to capture the sharpness of Paul's teaching.

Thus: could Paul have said that in appointing him to his service God had deemed him faithful (v. 12)? Did Paul think of faith (or faithfulness) as a qualification for work in quite that sense? Both this use of the word and the steadiness of character which it expresses are closer to the mentality of this writer (see the qualities required of his church officers in ch. 3) than that of Paul. Then, would Paul have said that he had *received mercy* from God in his appointment to his service because he had *acted ignorantly in unbelief* (v. 13)? The impression is that God overlooked Paul's apparent unsuitability for the post (as in the rest of the letter, we are almost in a world where we can speak of church employment), because there was the extenuating circumstance that in opposing Christ he had acted in ignorance. How fair-minded of God! And how remote we are from the Pauline dynamic of total unworthiness and free unmerited grace. The other motive for the tolerance accorded to Paul is Jesus Christ's *patience* (*makrothumia*); and it was displayed in the case of Paul in order that other Christians might also be encouraged. Again, it is hardly a Pauline way of looking at the work of God for man's salvation. It is true that *makrothumia* appears as a quality of God in Rom. 2[4] and 9[22] (cf. 3[25]), but it is in connection with the wide sweep of his dealings with the human race not the close and intimate relationship of grace. It is presented not, as in our passage, as an encouragement to those who are embarking on the Christian life but as a warning and an explanation to those who remain outside it. Moreover, *mercy* here seems to be almost identical with *patience*: it is a quality of God's quiet, static, long-term existence rather than his vigorous, dynamic saving work.

At a cursory glance, these shifts in sense may seem small. In fact, they are symptoms of the crucial change which occurred between the life of Paul and the work of his imitator. German theology speaks of it as a shift from 'spirit' to 'office'; that is, from a concern with the direct relationship of God with man for salvation to a concern with the organization and structure of the Church as an institution. The shift was no doubt partly the result of the lower calibre of the later writer, partly the result of the failure of the expected End of the world to materialize, and partly the result of the inevitable pressure of questions of the ordering of the Church. What is interesting in our present passage, which is not ostensibly related to these questions at all, is the way in which the writer, no doubt unconsciously, sees the disposition of God himself reflecting the qualities and attitudes to which he attaches so much importance in the affairs of the Church on earth.

Paul is not only made rather banal. In one respect our passage contains a positive travesty of his teaching. Once more the pressures of the times may well be the explanation. V. 8 takes a positive and high view of the law (and states it almost tautologously!). Now there are passages in undoubted Paul which can be quoted in the same sense. Rom. 7¹², though it uses adjectives different from that in our passage (*kalos*), makes the same point. But we miss here all trace of the subtlety and paradox which characterize Paul's teaching about law, all sense of its varied roles and qualities. Instead we have a plain point, plainly put. And when our writer says (v. 9) that *the law is not laid down for the just* (*dikaios*), he uses the word by which Paul designates the justified man, the one who has been wonderfully acquitted of Sin by God's sheer grace, but he means by it, more straightforwardly and prosaically, simply the law-abiding man. This is not to suggest that Paul himself was unconcerned about moral obedience: cf. Rom. 13⁸⁻¹⁰; II Cor. 5¹⁰, for example. It is to maintain that Paul's teaching on the relationship between man's standing in relation to God and his moral duty was much more subtle and complex than that of our writer, for whom the law is what it was in Judaism, the guide for life.

But what can he mean by *the law* (v. 8)? Surely he cannot mean what Paul would almost certainly have meant in such a context, that is, the Jewish Law. Writing to a Christian audience some fifty years after Paul's death, he must surely mean the moral teaching accepted by Christians. And the fact that he can use the term without explanation or qualification is itself an indication of how far the Church has travelled since Paul's day. Not only has it lost the edge of his teaching on this matter (perhaps that was inevitable); it has now developed its own moral system, as it were alongside that of Judaism and no doubt other schools of thought in the contemporary society, and can refer to it quite simply as 'the law'. To judge from the following verses, it was, by comparison with Judaism, a moral rather than also a ceremonial law. That change at least had been permanently achieved by Paul in his mission to Gentiles.

The transformation of Paul into a pure moralist reaches its climax in v. 11, where the ethical commonplaces which have just been listed are identified as the substance of *the glorious gospel*. The Paul who wrote Rom. 1¹⁶ would hardly have seen it thus (though cf. Rom. 2¹⁶, where the Day of Judgement is *part* of Paul's gospel).

It is easy to decry this shift of emphasis and to see it as a decline from a pristine faith. However valid such a judgement may be religiously, it needs to be balanced by an effort of historical sympathy. The writer of the Pastoral Epistles may indeed have lacked Paul's depth but he was responding to the needs of the Church of his day – a need to sustain high moral standards and to resist moves towards antinomianism accompanied by heady religious fervour. He may have had a more distinctly polemical purpose: to counter those who claimed the name of Paul for such policies and attitudes. If Paul were not to become the property of such men, he must be seen as the patron of a more sober and firmly grounded faith. This passage opens the case for such an account of Paul.

3

going to Macedonia: it is hard to know whether it is misplaced effort to attempt to fit this and other geographical and personal information in the Pastoral Epistles into our other evidence concerning Paul's life (cf. p. 34). The effort may be misplaced for two reasons. First, because the account given in Acts may well be, to a greater or lesser degree, arranged by the author in accordance with his various narrative and religious principles, leaving us, as reliable evidence, only the meagre and problematic details to be found in the genuine epistles. Second, because our author may not have intended his statements to correspond with any evidence known to him. If we reject the hypothesis that passages like this are fragments of genuine Pauline writing (cf. p. 33), we should certainly entertain the possibility just mentioned. They were designed to convey verisimilitude to readers less apt to weigh up various sources of evidence than are modern biblical scholars.

If the effort is nevertheless made, it is hard to win for it any reward. The undoubted epistles afford no relevant evidence, unless we make the unlikely assumption that I and II Timothy were written at widely differing times. For II Timothy is set at the end of Paul's life (4[6ff.]); and the only position for the journey referred to in I Tim. 1[3] known from the genuine letters is that mentioned in I Cor. 16[5]. Together with v. 8 of the same chapter, could that have been the basis on which our writer constructs his little piece of verisimilitude? V. 8 speaks of Paul remaining (cf. I Tim. 1[3]) in Ephesus until his travelling starts – which could be supposed not to be before Timothy's return, foreseen in v. 11. Then Timothy will in turn *remain at Ephesus.* If our writer used I

Corinthians (which was, we know, among the best known of Paul's epistles in these early decades), and used it thus (in a manner so sloppy from the point of view of anyone interested in fitting together a total picture of Paul's career), then we need not be surprised that the evidence of Acts has no useful bearing on our passage. Indeed, not only may Acts be less than strictly historical, it may not have been known to our writer and may not even have been written when he was at work (cf. p. 24f.).

In Acts, there are two journeys to Macedonia. The first follows closely on the episode of Timothy's circumcision (16¹ff.,¹¹f.), and antedates Paul's activity in Ephesus. From 17¹⁴f., it may be inferred that Timothy actually accompanies Paul on this journey. In the case of the second visit (20¹), Timothy has gone ahead of Paul (19²²). Neither story can be pressed into any connection with our present passage.

to teach different doctrine: heterodidaskalein – a word found in Christian usage only, occurring also in Ignatius' Letter to Polycarp 3¹ (*ECW*, p. 128). That such a word should be formed indicates that concern of our writer with orthodoxy which his work makes abundantly clear. The concept was not in the forefront of the mind of the historical Paul, but the writer of this work claims his authority as he urges it upon his audience.

4

myths and endless genealogies: the most likely reference is to the speculative, luxuriant, even vertiginous theological and cosmological constructions which came to their full flowering among the Gnostic sects of the second century A.D. This writer is as far removed as possible from them by both temperament and conviction. His religion is moral in emphasis, sober in tone. Only in 3¹⁶ (almost certainly a quotation) does he even approach the kind of pattern which the myth-makers would have found congenial; though the ideas behind 2¹³f. might merit the label 'speculative', at least from the modern commentator. It would be unjust to saddle our plain and sober Pastoral Epistle writer with all the associations which plainness and sobriety in theology have for us.

As to the content of the terms, *myths* and *genealogies* clearly belong together – indeed, there is enough evidence to indicate that the pair made a conventional phrase. There is no need then to distinguish oversharply between the two words. The reference to *Jewish myths* in Tit. 1¹⁴ and to *genealogies* alongside *quarrels over the law* in Tit. 3⁹ is our next pointer to their proper interpretation. If second century Gnosticism was the fulfilment of the process whose earlier stages we witness here, our writer is concerned with its Jewish rather than its pagan roots. As sources as disparate as Philo and the Dead Sea Scrolls indicate, Judaism was at this time capable of spawning rich theological speculation, much of it taking its rise from the stories and genealogical material in Genesis. The biblical stories were developed into new but derivative tales – and *myths* (*muthoi*) was the precise term for such tales on the lips of one who disapproved of them.* As for *genealogies*, Philo can speak of the narrative parts of the Pentateuch as 'the genealogical (writing)'.† And in the Qumran *Manual of Discipline*, we read: 'This is for the man who would bring others to the inner vision, so that he may understand and teach to all the children of light the real nature of men, touching ... their actions throughout their generations' (1QS III$^{13f.}$). Our writer would probably have found such esoteric ways objectionable.‡

In Paul's lifetime, Jewish teaching of this early Gnostic character had already appeared as a challenge. This is almost certainly the enemy in Colossians,§ but two changes have occurred. The Colossian troubles seem to be caused by Jews outside not inside the Church: the Synagogue is attacking its novel offshoot. Now the concern is with people of Jewish provenance within the Church. Second, Paul's own teaching in Colossians (e.g. 1$^{15-20}$) might well have struck our writer as culpably speculative. It certainly contrasts sharply with the prosaic tone of most of the Pastoral Epistles.

training: some MSS have a similar Greek word (*oikodomē* rather than *oikonomia*), which yields the nice contrast – solid building rather than insubstantial speculation. The better attested *oikonomia* may mean *training* (as RSV), a sense fully in line with the writer's attitudes – he sees Christian life as a disciplined process; or else it may carry the sense of 'plan' and refer to God's saving purpose for his people (cf. Eph. 1^{10}; 3^{2,9}). In that case the contrast is between the authentic and bogus accounts of divine saving action.

5

aim ... is love: the writer's strong moral purpose immediately appears. As the rest of this passage shows, he cares about this at least as much as

* *The Book of Jubilees* is one of the most familiar examples of this work. Charles, II, p. 1ff.

†Vit. Mos. 2$^{45-7}$, see F. H. Colson and C. H. Whitaker (eds.), *Philo*, vol. IV, Heinemann, 1929, p. 471.

‡For the Jewish origins of Gnosticism, see R. M. Grant, *Gnosticism and Early Christianity*, Oxford University Press, 1960.

§cf. J. L. Houlden, *Paul's Letters from Prison*, Penguin, 1970, p. 122ff.

orthodoxy of belief. Even *faith* is morally directed, by the addition of the adjective *sincere* – more strongly than in the comparable Pauline statement in Gal. 5⁶. The fact that *charge* (*paraggelia*) takes up the verb used in v. 3 may mean that it refers to this specific instruction rather than the preaching in general. *Pure heart*: cf. Ps. 24 (LXX 23)⁴; Matt. 5⁸; II Tim. 2²².

The three phrases which end this verse, giving the qualities which give rise to love, are stock expressions for this writer: cf. (with variations) I Tim. 1¹⁹; 3⁹; II Tim. 1³,⁵; 2²²; Tit. 2¹⁴. Often two of them are combined. All three express a single idea: solid sincerity of purpose is the basis of virtue, and the heart of virtue is love (cf. Mark 12²⁸⁻³⁴; Rom. 13⁸ff.).

good conscience: it might be thought that this would issue from loving behaviour rather than the reverse. But for our writer a smooth and well-grounded moral integrity, including an unclouded conscience, is a prerequisite for good action. It may be seen as a tamed equivalent of Paul's justification by faith (cf. *faith* at the end of the verse). But for Paul, man's good acts spring from acceptance and freedom conferred by God's generosity, whereas here attention centres on man's own moral power.

Perhaps it is then not surprising that the phrase *good conscience* does not appear in genuine Paul. *Conscience* (*suneidēsis*) in Greek means first consciousness of oneself, then, commonly, an inner consciousness of evil, a sense of having failed morally. This is the usual meaning in Paul. Its use to signify a neutral moral guide is not found. There is therefore a secondary and derivative quality about the expression *good conscience*. It means the absence of the painful sense of failure. Comparable expressions occur in Philo and in Ignatius (Mag. 4; Philad. 6³), and, in the New Testament, the phrase itself is found in Acts 23¹; I Peter 3¹⁶,²¹; cf. Acts 24¹⁶, as well as the passages in the Pastoral Epistles already mentioned. It comes into these later New Testament writings almost certainly from current Hellenistic usage, and, as our present passage shows, is placed 'among fundamental presuppositions of a peaceful Christian life'.*

6

certain persons: typical of contemporary polemical style, cf. 1¹⁹; 6¹⁰,²¹; Heb. 10²⁵; I Clem. 1¹.

*Conzelmann, *Commentary*, p. 20. See also C. A. Pierce, *Conscience in the New Testament*, SCM, 1955.

swerving ... wandered away: both common words in these writings. The first, *astochein*, appears again in 6²¹ and II Tim. 2¹⁸. The former passage retains in RSV its leading sense – to miss the mark. The second, *ektrepomai*, occurs in 5¹⁵; 6²⁰ and II Tim. 4⁴. Both express well the writer's concern with the straight path of correct belief. More accurately, they express his more notable concern with the straightness of the path than with the actual content of either right or wrong belief – both of which he fails to describe in any detail. Heresy is simply denigrated as 'foolish talk' (RSV, *vain discussion, mataiologia*); cf. Tit. 1¹⁰.

7

teachers of the law: what does *the law* signify here? To judge from v. 4, it is used in the wider Jewish sense of the Torah, the Pentateuch, as a whole – not only its moral and ceremonial provisions, and their elaboration, but also its narrative element and *its* elaboration (cf. *myths and genealogies*, v. 4). Yet in v. 8ff. it is clear that *the law* refers exclusively to moral provisions. The shift in sense reflects our writer's opinions. As a Hellenistic Christian, he is wary of both the ceremonial and the legendary aspects of the Torah which were part and parcel of the whole to the Jewish Christians whom he attacks. (Jewish scribes of the time would be skilled in all these areas.) For his down to earth version of Gentile Christianity, *the law* means the basic moral provisions – in fact the commonplaces of all moral systems – whose infringers he lists.

9ff.

law is not ... for the just: the distinction made here could hardly come from the pen of Paul. The fact that it could not illustrates well the difference between his concept of law and this writer's. For Paul law was not simply a collection of moral rules. It was rather a dispensation under which, at its widest, all men live. It broods over all and condemns all: Rom. 1¹⁹; 2¹⁵; 3¹⁹,²³. Law for our writer signifies not a spiritual regime but the rules by which citizens live. As in v. 8 (see above, p. 53), where Paul's bold statement (Rom. 7¹²) that the law is good is larded with caution, the paradoxical and wide-sweeping quality of Paul's teaching is lost.

the lawless etc: the list contains the most outrageous offences in the estimation of the contemporary world. The form of such catalogues is more typical of Hellenistic than rabbinic moral writing (in the New Testament, cf. Rom. 1²⁹⁻³¹; Col. 3⁵), but the content of this list shows

the influence of the Decalogue, at least from *murderers of fathers* onwards (Ex. 20¹²). (There is evidence of Jews thinking of kidnapping as
a particularly heinous example of the sin of theft, under the eighth
commandment.) For the general conclusion, cf. Rom. 13⁹; Gal. 5²¹.

Two words are particularly characteristic of this writer: *the ungodly*
(*asebeis*) introduces a family of words common in the Pastoral Epistles
(and, within the New Testament, those other late writings, II Peter and
Jude). *Eusebeia*, the positive noun in the family, occurring first in 2²,
signifies 'piety'. It is one of the leading qualities which form the common ground of esteem shared by these Christians, Hellenistic Judaism
and respectable paganism: it was a virtue greatly approved at this time
and its use is a small sign that in these letters we are moving from a
Christianity which is wholly on the crest of the wave into a degree of
acceptance of a pluralist society. In the LXX, the great majority of
occurrences are in the late book, IV Maccabees. The other typical word
is *sound* (from *hugiainō*). It comes eight times in these letters (never in
Paul) and again illustrates the writer's values.

13
blasphemed and persecuted: three of Paul's genuine letters allude to his
activity against the Church before his conversion, cf. I Cor. 15⁹; Gal.
1¹³; Phil. 3⁶. In any attempt to give biographical verisimilitude, a
reference to this fact about Paul was bound to receive a place. cf. also
Acts 7⁵⁸; 8¹; 9¹.

14
overflowed: the allusion to I Cor. 15⁹ᶠ· is continued with this reference
to the abundance of God's grace. As we have seen (p. 52f.), other
features of this passage lead the reader to question how far the writer,
who follows Paul's personal statement at this point, has fully absorbed
the depth of his theology.

faith and love: have become a conventional pair, cf. I Cor. 13¹³; Gal.
5⁶; I Thess. 3⁶.
in Christ Jesus: seems to lack the full mystical sense of this language in
Paul and to mean rather that these qualities are marks of Christian life
(cf. p. 27).

15
the saying is sure: (lit. 'faithful' or, better here, 'trustworthy') this
phrase (*pistos ho logos*) is a favourite with our writer and is used by no
other New Testament writer. It appears also in 3¹ (some textual doubt,

see notes); 4^9; II Tim. 2^{11}; Tit. 3^8. Sometimes it follows, sometimes precedes, the saying to which it refers. It is used to draw attention to key doctrinal statements, especially, it seems, concerning the life to come (though this may not apply to the present passage or, at least as set out in RSV, to 3^1). This is perhaps a measure of the importance to this writer of right doctrine concerning this matter.

Why is the formula used? In some cases, it may be to mark an already traditional doctrinal affirmation. Our present verse looks like an example; so does II Tim. 2^{11}, where what is almost certainly a quotation follows. But I Tim. 3^1 and Tit. 3^7 do not (though the latter may, perhaps from v. 3 on); and even if the former refers to the preceding verse about Eve rather than the instructions about bishops, the case is not greatly helped. Moreover, there are likely quotations (e.g. I Tim. 3^{16}) which are not marked out by this formula. It is best to say that the writer uses this phrase to designate certain chiefly doctrinal affirmations which he considers to be of central significance. Perhaps some of them were cherished and often used statements of his own teaching. As for the formula itself, there are one or two parallels in Jewish literature of the period; cf. also Rev. 21^5 and 22^6.

If the 'trustworthy saying' is taken from Christian tradition, then it stops at *sinners*. The rest of the verse is reminiscent of I Cor. 15^9 and links us back to v. 13f.

save sinners: in Paul this verb usually refers to the ultimate 'safety' to be given by God on the Last Day, though already in train for his people. It is commonly in the passive. In these writings its reference is more general. It occurs seven times, and refers most obviously to the future in I Tim. 2^{15}; 4^{16}; II Tim. 4^{18}; and clearly to an accomplished act in II Tim. 1^9 and Tit. 3^5. Only in II Tim. 4^{18} does it refer with complete clarity to the coming age after the End or perhaps, more simply, the future life which follows death (for the former, cf. Tit. 2^{13}).

It is doubtful whether the reference to Jesus' *coming* into the world implies, at any rate for the writer's thought, a fully articulate doctrine of Christ's pre-existence (cf. also II Tim. 1^{10}). That belief may, however, be implied in I Tim. 3^{16} – almost certainly a quotation and not the writer's own composition.

16

eternal life: the phrase recurs in 6^{12} and in Tit. 1^2 and 3^7, cf. I Tim. 4^8. It is not clear whether this writer fully adopts (though in christianized form) the usual scheme of Jewish chronology and eschatology – a division of time into the present age and the age to come, with 'eternal life' (lit. 'the life of the age', *aiōn*) as the term for existence in the second great epoch. Two passages (II Tim. 4[8] and Tit. 2[13]) support the view that he does adopt this scheme, and that the phrase does not refer simply to life after death. But I Tim. 4[8] shows that the awareness of 'life' from God, so vivid and full-blooded in the Christian consciousness of Paul as a gift here and now, has lost some of its strength and power (cf. Rom. 5[10]; 8[2]; Gal. 2[20]); contrast, however, 6[12]. cf. p. 107.

17

For the doxology, cf. 6[15f.]; Rom. 11[36]; 16[25-7]; Gal. 1[5]. *King of ages*: for the sense, cf. v. 16 above. For the title, cf. Tobit 13[7,11]; I Clem. 61[2]; and Rev. 15[3] (text doubtful). The parallel in Tobit confirms the Jewish origins of the phrase. The following adjectives, on the other hand, though by no means strange to the thought of Hellenistic Judaism, owe something to the stock ideas of common pagan philosophy. For *invisible*, cf. Heb. 11[27]. For the whole set of attributes, cf. 6[16].

18

charge: looks back to v. 3ff.

commit: the corresponding noun occurs in 6[20]; II Tim. 1[12,14]; and the verb again in II Tim. 2[2]. It is then an important word for our writer. This is because it expresses the solemnity of the commissioning of the officers of the Church whose vital task is that preservation of the true faith which the writer feels to be so much under threat.

my son: cf. v. 2.

prophetic utterances: a reference not to the prophetic oracles of the Old Testament, but to Spirit-inspired activity in the Church whereby speech was uttered and decisions made under the guidance of God: cf. Acts 13[1f.]; I Cor. 14[1-3]. A particularly vivid example of the working of prophecy in the Church at this time is to be found in Ignatius, Philad. 7: 'I cried out, speaking with a loud voice – the very voice of God – "Be loyal to your bishop and clergy and deacons". Some who were there suspected me of saying this because I already knew of certain dissensions among you; but he whose prisoner I am will bear me witness that no such information had ever reached me from human lips. No; that was the preaching of the Spirit itself' (*ECW*, p. 113). Like our present passage, this quotation shows the role of prophecy in connection with the establishing of proper authority in the hands of

authentic leaders. The orthodox leadership is validated by nothing less
than the inspiration of God himself. It was a matter of central importance for the writer of these works and close to the heart of his purpose;
cf. I Tim. 4¹⁴.

the good warfare: cf. Eph. 6¹¹ᶠᶠ·; I Tim. 6¹²; II Tim. 2³ᶠ·; 4⁷. The military
image was common and widespread in religious groups at the time.

19
their faith: lit. 'the faith', i.e. Christianity, as commonly in these
writings.

20
Hymenaeus and Alexander: the former reappears in II Tim. 2¹⁷, the
latter in II Tim. 4¹⁴. A decision about the authenticity of these names
depends on a general judgement on this aspect of the Pastoral Epistles.
On the other hand, such details are part of the *prima facie* evidence for
that judgement; they are almost impossible to assess (see p. 33f.).

delivered to Satan: cf. I Cor. 5⁵. The rest of the verse makes it seem that
some kind of discipline, perhaps involving temporary exclusion from
the congregation, is in mind. Outside the circle of God's faithful,
Satan still rules.

2¹⁻¹⁵   PRAYER – CONTENTS AND MANNER

1 *First of all, then, I urge that supplications, prayers, intercessions, and
thanksgiving be made for all men,* 2 *for kings and all who are in high
positions, that we may lead a quiet and peaceable life, godly and respectful
in every way.* 3 *This is good, and it is acceptable in the sight of God our
Saviour,* 4 *who desires all men to be saved and to come to the knowledge of
the truth.* 5 *For there is one God, and there is one mediator between God
and men, the man Christ Jesus,* 6 *who gave himself as a ransom for all, the
testimony to which was borne at the proper time.* 7 *For this I was appointed
a preacher (I am telling the truth, I am not lying), a teacher of the Gentiles
in faith and truth.*
8 *I desire then that in every place the men should pray, lifting holy hands
without anger or quarrelling;* 9 *also that women should adorn themselves*

modestly and sensibly in seemly apparel, not with braided hair or gold or pearls or costly attire ¹⁰ *but by good deeds, as befits women who profess religion.* ¹¹ *Let a woman learn in silence with all submissiveness.* ¹² *I permit no woman to teach or to have authority over men; she is to keep silent.* ¹³ *For Adam was formed first, then Eve;* ¹⁴ *and Adam was not deceived, but the woman was deceived and became a transgressor.* ¹⁵ *Yet woman will be saved through bearing children*ᶜ, *if she continues*ᵈ *in faith and love and holiness, with modesty.*

ᶜOr *by birth of the child*   ᵈGreek *they continue*

At first sight, this passage marks an abrupt break with what has preceded it. Heresy threatens and properly designated authority must combat it. We might expect to receive an exposition of true doctrine at this point. Instead we have practical instruction on the prayer and then, for most of the rest of the work, the organization of the community. But does not this accurately reveal the author's mind? For him, the right riposte to false teaching is the proper arranging of the congregation's life, in particular its worship and structure (cf. 3¹⁵). True, doctrinal statements come in (e.g. 2⁵), but they serve to back up the arrangements which occupy the centre of attention. If Church life is on a sound basis, then true doctrine will win its way.

It is not clear how polemical the present passage is (or indeed the following chapters). Are the persons referred to in 1⁴ inclined to worship which neglects the sober duty of prayer for the society in which the Church is placed, preferring more exciting and 'advanced' religious activity? Are they likewise inclined to tolerate what the writer would consider anarchic conditions in the organization of the Church (cf. ch. 3 and 5), and do they make unsuitable choices for posts of responsibility? Do they permit suitably inspired women to express themselves in the affairs and the meetings of the congregation (v. 8ff.)?

If these are indeed the tendencies of those opposed to the writer, then appealing to the patronage of Paul may well have been a game which both sides could play. That best known of Paul's letters, I Corinthians (so it appears from the number of early quotations from it), could plausibly be appealed to in support of precisely the states of affairs which our writer finds so hazardous. The enthusiastic free glossolalia discussed in ch. 14 and the implicit permission to women to speak at

Church meetings (11^5), together with the picture of a rich variety of spiritual activity given in ch. 12, could speak for the opponents' case. It is left to our writer, by explicit allusion (e.g. to I Cor. 14^{34} in 2^{11}) or by simply taking his own line, to witness to the other side of Paul's often judiciously balanced writing. The trouble with Paul (or rather his glory!) was that on so many issues he walked a delicate tightrope, along which it was hard for less agile successors to follow him. In any case, changed circumstances altered the shape of the discussion.

The bias of our writer is left in no doubt. Unlike Paul, he sees the Church not as a self-contained society with whom the future, on the cosmic scale, lies (I Cor. 6^3), but implicitly as only one element in society and, again implicitly, responsible alongside other men of good will (he might have coined the phrase) for keeping the fabric of society in being. In that sense, though his claims for Christianity are absolute (cf. v. 5), yet his sense of the Church's role is less so. Though he might not have admitted the validity of the prayers of others for the emperor, he was willing to share, perhaps grudgingly, with them in the task of upholding the authorities with spiritual support (as did the Roman Catholic Church in non-Roman Catholic countries before the Second Vatican Council).

It is the first verses of this chapter which particularly give these writings the reputation of being bourgeois in their outlook and assumptions. The charge is just; but it should not deny the writer our understanding. Though the hope of the return of Jesus in triumph and judgement is lively enough (II Tim. 4^8 and Tit. 2^{13}), every decade that elapsed without the realization of that hope meant if not its fading then at least an increasing need to adjust to life within ordinary and persisting human society. Paul himself, for whom the hope was intensely alive, could still pay attention to the duties imposed by man's political circumstances (Rom. $13^{1ff.}$) – but in the light of the coming End.* By the Pastoral Epistles, we have moved to a more settled perspective, to what we might call the first newspaper-reading generation of churchmen, those aware of some responsibility for society and interested in its affairs. The author of Acts belongs even more clearly to the same band. Yet of course, if bourgeois, then cer-

---

*See J. L. Houlden, *Ethics and the New Testament*, Penguin, 1973, p. 81; Jack T. Sanders, *Ethics in the New Testament*, SCM, 1976.

tainly *petit* bourgeois. The interest of this writer's circle is not to take part in public affairs or to direct them, but to *lead a quiet and peaceable life*, and, we may suppose, not to distinguish too keenly between good emperors and bad, but to support the existing powers so long as this minimum condition is fulfilled. In his eyes, God himself is content with government on these terms and asks no more (v. 3). What churchmen can provide is prayer not criticism.

This rather civic context provides the longest piece of teaching on prayer in the New Testament literature. In a passage like I Cor. 14, we witness Christians at prayer, but in conditions of such fervour that it was superfluous to expound the subject: they simply prayed. In the other significant passage on the subject, Matt. 6$^{5ff.}$, we find only the simple doctrine that prayer must be single-minded and directed towards the one end of the coming of the Kingdom. In our present passage, by contrast, we have the first extant instruction on the matter. Christians now needed to be taught what and how to pray.

As far as meetings of the Church are concerned, prayer is men's business, as in the synagogue. We have seen that the writer does no more than repeat (with a nice piece of scriptural embellishment) part at least of Paul's own doctrine on the matter of women's role on such occasions. But the scriptural allusion has the effect of giving to this judgement a strength which is lacking in Paul himself. Paul's doctrine is much more subtle. He had his reasons for the subordination of women in certain aspects of Church life. It seems that he considered it improper for them to bear rule in the outward affairs of the community or to speak except when inspired by the Spirit (I Cor. 11^5 – in other circumstances, women should keep their questions until they reach home, 14$^{34f.}$). But there was also the profound principle that in Christ 'there is neither male nor female' (Gal. 3^{28}) – a fundamental equality which I Tim. 2$^{13ff.}$ was not calculated to maintain.

I

supplications, etc.: the most general word comes second in the list. The first term signifies a more specific and personal request to God. *Intercession* is prayer on behalf of others.

for all men: perhaps linked particularly with the last two nouns – *intercessions* and *thanksgiving*. Not all Christian congregations at this time had this width of concern: I John, for example, shows no trace of it, cf. 5¹⁹. But see Ignatius, Eph. 10¹ (*ECW*, p. 78).

2

for kings: the word was used also for the Roman emperor (*basileus*), who was no doubt chiefly in mind. The plural has indeed been taken as evidence that the writing dates from after A.D. 137, when the imperial throne was shared, but it is perhaps more likely that the sense is general. The duty of prayer for rulers was widely recognized. Among Jews, see Ezra 6¹⁰; Pirke Aboth 3² (Charles, II, p. 698). Among Christians, I Clem. 6of. (*ECW*, p. 55); Epistle of Polycarp 12 (*ECW*, p. 149); cf. I Peter 2¹³⁻¹⁷, but contrast Rev. 14⁸. That Christians were willing to undertake it became in the second century an important point in Christian apologetic.* This motive is not apparent in our passage, but it was ready to enter the stage. As with Jews, it was a crucial sign of the loyalty of a group which would not take part in the cult of the emperor.

godly and respectful in every way: lit. 'in all piety and seriousness', which is better. These are both major virtues for this writer. For the former, cf. p. 59. The latter appears again in 3⁴ and Tit. 2².

3

Saviour: cf. 1¹, p. 47.

4

all men to be saved: if the ideal of life is to exist in 'all piety and moral seriousness', as v. 2 says, it is fair to ask whether the salvation here desired for all men is quite as radical as other New Testament writings and general Christian usage would suggest. We have little hint here of man's predicament, as in the grip of sin and death (e.g. Rom. 6²⁰; 7²⁴), little sense of his transformation by God. Does the writer envisage instead for *all men* their avoidance of the gross evils listed in 1⁹ᶠ· and their acceptance of his scheme of values (together no doubt with his impressive but somewhat flat and unelaborated doctrinal statements), and is that what he sees as their way to salvation? That is to ask the question sharply. But if this at all represents the direction of his mind, the relevance of our passage to general Christian discussion of the question of universalism, often cast in the mould of a strongly Pauline dynamic, is

---

*cf. Athenagoras, 'A Plea Regarding Christians', ch. 37, *LCC*, I, London, 1953, p. 340.

softened. Again putting it over-sharply, his hope is for an increasingly
moral and tranquil society, living contentedly under God, rather than
the renewal of all things (Rom. 8$^{18ff.}$).

knowledge of the truth: i.e. the Christian faith. cf. II Tim. 2^{25}; 3^7; Tit. 1^1.
The use of this phrase serves to emphasize the openly accessible nature
of Christian faith and life. Reasonable men can grasp it (*epignōsis* probably implies active apprehension, not mere acquiring of information).
Another symptom that the world at large is now the stage on which
the Church lives.

5

one God: the assertion of monotheism was a leading point of Jewish
apologetic in relation to the pagan world, and Christians took it over
as an important part of their own statement of belief. There is another
example of it in Eph. 4^6, this time as the climax of a quasi-credal
formula; and Paul states it squarely in I Cor. 8$^{4-6}$, cf. Rom. 3^{30}. For
instances of this apologetic in homiletic form, cf. Acts 14^{15}; 17$^{24ff.}$.
Many pagans would have agreed, and in Acts 17^{28}, Paul is portrayed
appealing to pagan literature in support of his doctrine. Often dispute
turned not so much on whether there was one God or a plurality of
gods, as on the right way to understand the many deities of paganism:
were they all manifestations of a single deity, or no more than figures
in stories? or were they subordinate spiritual beings, and if so, were
they beneficent or malign, and should they be seen as angels or devils
(in Jewish and Christian terms)? cf. I Cor. 8^4; 10$^{19f.}$.* Though there is
no formal introduction – no use of the writer's phrase *the saying is sure*
(cf. 1^{15}, p. 59f.) – this verse and probably the following clause are a
familiar formula of the Church, perhaps used in worship or teaching.
Was it an adaptation by this Christian congregation of the Jewish
shema, Deut. 6^4? The fact that it is a set form is confirmed by its not
being integral to the argument of the passage: it simply takes up and
comments on the reference to God in v. 3.

one mediator: whether the formula is the composition of our writer or
not, the sufficiency of a single mediator between God and man is a
point against the Gnostic-type beliefs which he has attacked in 1^4. A
leading feature of those systems was the profusion of mediators: they
safeguarded the utter transcendence of the heart of deity and smoothed
the transition between 'it' and base matter.

*For a slightly later example, answering the pagan charge of atheism
(Christians denied the gods), see Justin's First Apology, 5f. (*LCC*, I, p. 244f.).

In the New Testament, *mediator* is not common. Its one Pauline use, in Gal. 3[19f.], refers to Moses, in his role as law-giver. It appears chiefly in Hebrews (8[6]; 9[15]; 12[24]), where Christ is compared implicitly with Moses: he is the mediator of the new and better covenant (cf. Ex. 24[1-11]). If in our present passage, the main thrust of the expression is anti-Gnostic – there is only one mediator and he is human not angelic – the tradition of thought is thoroughly Old Testament. There the idea of mediatorial figures between God and men (whether prophets, priests, or kings) abounds. Moses was pre-eminent among them, and our word, *mesitēs*, is used by Philo, writing in the first century A.D., chiefly of him (though he applies it also to angels). These figures were otherwise always human and though there were many of them they were generally seen to be in operation singly: this particular prophet, for example, now spoke the word of God.

However, the word itself occurs in the LXX only once: and the suggestion has arisen* that this occurrence, in Job 9[32f.], lies behind our passage. It offers an alternative, or additional, reason for the emphasis on Christ Jesus the mediator being a man. For in Job 9, the writer expresses a desire for a human mediator to be his spokesman to God. Job is a book little used by early Christian writers; but it so happens that it is drawn upon considerably in I Clement – which, as we have seen (p. 66), has similarities with I Timothy, particularly the immediately preceding verses, concerning prayer.

If 2[5f.] is an existing Church formula rather than our writer's composition, the evaluation of this possible connection is uncertain. At most, it might indicate a common provenance for the two works, i.e. Rome, the known source of I Clement. This, rather than literary dependence, would best take account of a shared interest in Job.

6

ransom: antilutron. The comparison is naturally made with Mk. 10[45] (where, however, we find the simpler form *lutron*, and a different preposition is used); cf. also Tit. 2[14], which uses the cognate verb and helps to show the imagery in mind. The basic idea is that of freeing slaves, but the concept of purificatory sacrifice is close at hand. The crucial episode of the Exodus from Egypt, when, after the smearing of the doors with the blood of the Passover lambs, the Israelites were freed from their bondage, probably lies in the background. There may even be a conscious reference to the Marcan passage or to a saying of Jesus which lies behind it. Those who accept dependence on an older

* A. T. Hanson, *Studies in the Pastoral Epistles*, SPCK, 1968, pp. 56–64.

formulation such as that in Mark and who believe this to represent very early tradition see in these verses the combining of a Hellenistic formula (v. 5), concerning the status of Christ and mildly philosophical in tone, with a much older Palestinian statement speaking of him in terms of his work.*

testimony ... at the proper time: the RSV is speculative. Literally, 'the testimony in its own time'. The phrase is best taken as describing Christ's act of self-giving, which is seen as having happened at the time designed in God's plan of salvation, and as witnessing to that plan before mankind.

7

preacher: lit. 'herald', *kērux*. cf. II Tim. 1[11]. Both Jews and pagans could use the word in our present sense. It does not occur in genuine Paul. But for the rest of the verse, cf. Rom. 9[1]; I Cor. 9[1]; 15[9f.]; Gal. 1[20]; 2[7ff.]. It resumes the reminiscence of autobiographical statements concerning the basis of Paul's authority which we observed first in 1[13]. Eph. 3[7] contains another example of the same kind of statement, given for the same purpose – to support the authority of the imitator. The very strength of the language constitutes near proof of pseudonymity: the historical Timothy, Paul's close associate, would hardly have required assurances of this sort.

8

I desire: boulomai carries a sense of legislative enactment – 'it is my pleasure'; cf. 5[14].

in every place: this expression, odd here, may be an allusion to Mal. 1[11], a much quoted verse in the early Church, cf. Didache 14 (*ECW*, p. 234), which also has the theme of purity, see below.

the men should pray: returning to the theme of prayer with which the chapter began, but now considering manner rather than content, the writer shows himself in favour of the Church simply taking over the custom of the synagogue (cf. p. 66), where vocal prayer was the business of males (cf. v. 11).

holy hands: hosios (holy) instead of the much commoner *hagios* (only nine times in the New Testament). Though the two words shade into

*See David Hill, *Greek Words and Hebrew Meanings*, Cambridge University Press, 1967, p. 76f.

each other, *hosios* tends to mean 'pious', 'devout', while *hagios* is the more cultic word – 'sacred'. The expression, *holy hands*, in a sense that is partly moral, partly ritual, is common in both Jewish and pagan sources. Here and in subsequent Christian use, the stress lies on the moral side, as the following phrase shows.

The conventional attitude of prayer is referred to: standing with hands outstretched: cf. I Clem. 2: 'You would stretch out suppliant hands to Almighty God' (*ECW*, p. 24).

without anger: a strong emphasis in early Christianity, cf. Matt. 6[14]; Eph. 4[26].

9

women ... adorn themselves: other early Christian congregations had the same feeling about the propriety of women's self-adornment, cf. I Peter 3[3]. So did pagan groups, e.g. concerning 'holy women' in the mystery religions. Chastity is the main object in view, as we can see from the positive extended treatment of at least some women's place in the Church in ch. 5. cf. also Isaiah 3[18-24].

sensibly: lit. 'with good sense' or 'decency'. The same word, *sōphrosunē*, a typical reflection of our writer's values, occurs again in v. 15 (RSV *with modesty*). The qualities admired in these verses are commonplace in the literature of the time, pagan and Jewish as well as Christian, when discussing feminine virtue.

These counsels begin by referring to women attending meetings for prayer, but clearly extend to life in general. Like many other elements in these letters, they probably come from the stock of catechetical material which these Christians shared with others and which they had simply taken over from the established morality of Jewish and pagan groups in the world around them. The very general word in v. 10 for *religion* (*theosebeia*, lit. 'worship of God') is one symptom of this: it lacks any particular Christian reference. This is its only appearance in the New Testament.

10

good deeds: a common phrase in these writings, cf. 3[1]; 5[10,25]; 6[18]; II Tim. 2[21]; 3[17]; Tit. 2[7,14]; 3[1,8,14]. Its prominence implies no formal antagonism to Paul's insistence on faith rather than works as the basis for man's true relationship with God. Rather, the issue which moved Paul is simply not raised here. Our writer is concerned with the behaviour of established Christians (cf. Rom. 3[20,27f.]).

11f.

The first statement reflects I Cor. 14³⁵, the second I Cor. 11³ᶠᶠ· where its reference is general: here, at least the primary concern is with gatherings for worship and teaching.

13–15

These verses place our writer in the world of Jewish speculative theology; or perhaps they should be judged as a special excursion into it, for it is the only example in these writings of this kind of elaboration of stories in the Pentateuch, so much beloved in Judaism at this period (*haggadah*, Heb. 'narrative'; distinguished from *halakah*, the elaboration of legal material).

The passage is related to contemporary Jewish exegesis of Gen. 3¹⁶⁻¹⁹, but two difficulties arise: the dating of some of the comparable passages in Jewish sources, and the precise reference of certain words in our passage and some of its parallels. The basic theme, the inferiority and gullibility of women, is a commonplace of the time, shared, as we have seen, by Paul (though with important modifications, cf. p. 65). But what of the treatment of the Genesis story?

Much turns on the interpretation of *deceived*, v. 14. In the first case, the word is the simple verb, *apataō*, in the second, the compound *exapataō*. The latter does not occur in the LXX, and it is the former word which appears in Gen. 3¹³. By the second century A.D., and perhaps earlier, it was taken in some Egyptian Christian circles to bear its sense of sexual seduction, and the story was being interpreted in this way (see The Protevangelium of James 13¹ (Hennecke I, p. 381)): 'Has the story (of Adam) been repeated in me? For as Adam was (absent) in the hour of his prayer and the serpent came and found Eve alone and deceived her and defiled her, so also has it happened to me'. In the Jewish apocalyptic work, *The Book of the Secrets of Enoch*, dating probably from early in the Christian era, we find the same story: 'And (the devil) understood his condemnation ..., therefore he conceived thought against Adam, in such form that he entered and seduced Eve, but did not touch Adam'.★ Whether our writer knows of this tradition must remain uncertain: despite his use of two different words for the deceiving of Adam and that of Eve, we may doubt whether he intends any important distinction. Undoubtedly in circulation by our period was the work of Philo, who interprets the story in terms of deception. On the other hand, the conclusion (*woman will be saved through bearing children*), which, as far as evidence goes, is a piece of originality on the

★ 31⁶; cf. Charles, II, p. 451.

part of this writer, would make an appropriate balance to the idea that Eve's sin consisted in yielding to the sexual wiles of the serpent.

II Cor.[11] also comes into the discussion. It may well be the case that our writer is using and developing this passage (vv. 1–3, 14): like II Tim. 2[14] and unlike the LXX of Gen. 3, Paul uses the compound verb for *deceived*. It is just possible that the story of the devil's transformation into an angel (v. 14) implies the seduction story, but neither here nor in its Jewish parallels is there explicit reference to sexual seduction.★

In any case, as we have already seen, our version of the tradition has its own special features. In addition to the idea of women's salvation being brought about through child-bearing, there is the idea – crucially different from Paul's doctrine – that theological capital is to be made from the detail in the story (and it is not really fair to the story!) that *Adam was not deceived*. For Paul's teaching, it is of central importance that Adam sinned and that he stands for all mankind, male and female alike (Rom. 5[12ff.] and I Cor. 15[22]). It is yet another example of the relative theological shallowness of our writer; though admittedly his main concern here is practical rather than doctrinal.

woman will be saved through bearing children: there are obscurities here. First, *woman* does not appear in the Greek. So what is the subject? Surely the reference is not to Eve, as in v. 14, but, by way of the use of *the woman* in that verse, to women in general (as in v. 9ff.); or rather, as the conditional clause implies, to Christian women. In that case, a second obscurity is cleared up: the salvation referred to must mean not physical safe-keeping in childbirth but that assured on the Last Day (cf. 2[4]; 4[16]; II Tim. 4[18]; Tit. 2[14]) – a salvation reserved for God's people who qualify by means of the belief and conduct which these letters so strongly encourage. Nevertheless, the means by which that salvation is to be attained is strange – unless it is seen as a counteracting of the means by which the Fall occurred (see above), or perhaps as including not just the bearing but also the rearing of children, cf. 5[10]; Tit. 2[4]. It would be within this writer's way of thought (and an interesting indication of his legislating for a Church which had come to stay) to see the bringing up of new recruits for the Church as woman's primary contribution to the cause. (Some see in v. 15 a reference to Mary and the birth of Christ, but this is most improbable.)

A third difficulty lies in the verb *continue:* the subject is 'they'. Unless we are to suppose an abrupt and ungrammatical change from singular to plural, this must refer to the children. In that case, the interpretation

★e.g. The Book of Adam and Eve, chs. 9–11, Charles, II, p. 136.

just suggested, giving a wider sense to the bearing of children, is supported. It is they who are to continue in faith, etc.

faith and love: cf. 1¹⁴; p. 59.   *modesty*: cf. v. 9, p. 70.

3¹⁻¹³   OVERSEERS AND SERVANTS OF THE CHURCH

¹ *The saying is sure: If any one aspires to the office of bishop, he desires a noble task.* ² *Now a bishop must be above reproach, the husband of one wife, temperate, sensible, dignified, hospitable, an apt teacher,* ³ *no drunkard, not violent but gentle, not quarrelsome, and no lover of money.* ⁴ *He must manage his own household well, keeping his children submissive and respectful in every way;* ⁵ *for if a man does not know how to manage his own household, how can he care for God's church?* ⁶ *He must not be a recent convert, or he may be puffed up with conceit and fall into the condemnation of the devil*ᵉ; ⁷ *moreover he must be well thought of by outsiders, or he may fall into reproach and the snare of the devil*ᶠ.

⁸*Deacons likewise must be serious, not double-tongued, not addicted to much wine, not greedy for gain;* ⁹ *they must hold the mystery of the faith with a clear conscience.* ¹⁰ *And let them also be tested first; then if they prove themselves blameless let them serve as deacons.* ¹¹ *The women likewise must be serious, no slanderers, but temperate, faithful in all things.* ¹² *Let deacons be the husband of one wife, and let them manage their children and their households well;* ¹³ *for those who serve well as deacons gain a good standing for themselves and also great confidence in the faith which is in Christ Jesus.*

ᵉOr *slanderer*

In the title to this section, we speak of 'overseers and servants of the Church'. RSV, on the other hand, says 'bishops' and 'deacons' (Greek *episkopos* and *diakonos*). The difference between the two pairs of words confronts us with the first question raised by this crucial part of I Timothy. How are we to evaluate the personages whose role is outlined here? Is it fair to use already the special Christian terms, 'bishop' and 'deacon', or is such technicality anachronistic? It may after all be alleged that to use these titles for these early officers of the congregation creates too strong an impression of smooth continuity between those days and our own. It may prevent our asking with sufficient rigour how much is shared by these men and the bishops of the Church today, and indeed the bishops in the long centuries between.

The astonishing thing is that in many respects the list of qualities given in this passage matches well the aspirations associated with the clerical office in modern times, especially in the Protestant churches since the Reformation. This reflects not only the pervasive influence of these writings themselves (for example in the Ordinal in the Anglican *Book of Common Prayer*), but also – closer to our immediate purpose – the degree to which Church life had already settled into a certain mould by the time these writings came into existence. After all, the emphases could have been quite different: these verses say nothing about cultic functions (but cf. 4^{13}), make no mention of self-authenticating charismatic gifts, do not refer to fervent evangelistic preaching. To go no further, we may doubt whether Paul would have emphasized precisely this set of requirements. Like these writings as a whole, they are evidence that we have reached a time when the Church is setting a high value on stable and peaceful congregational life and therefore values highly the leadership which will perpetuate it. To this end, its officers are beginning to acquire proper status. They are even being paid, cf. 5^{17}. 'Overseers' and 'servants' are a shade too general and untechnical, even if 'bishops' and 'deacons' are a shade too formal and specialized.

The tendencies witnessed in this passage and throughout these documents can be paralleled in other early Christian writings. Not surprisingly, the late first and early second centuries saw the emergence in many congregations of a more formal structure. There were variations of both arrangement and role, but the broad picture is identical. Even among the churches in which our writer is interested, it looks as if there was not complete uniformity: in this passage, the reference is to the single 'bishop' at the head of the congregation, whereas in Tit. 1$^{5ff.}$ it looks as if a body of elders is in charge. (But see the discussion on p. 142.) Also, in the former case there is a greater degree of 'professionalization'. Whereas the elders may well still be what their title suggests, the senior men of the congregation, that is, its natural leaders, a young man may be chosen as bishop (I Tim. 4^{12});

and he will be selected not because of any remarkable or miraculous charisma but because of his personal qualities and abilities, though his actual designation for office might be achieved by inspirational means rather then by discussion of his competence (cf. 1^{18} and 4^{14}). (We assume that 'Timothy' occupies the office described in this passage.)*

If we turn further afield, there is more variety. The Johannine Epistles give evidence of a less formal stage of development than our writings, but the movement is in the same direction even if the titles are different.† It is possible that the evidence of Acts (such as it is) should be taken to bear on the author's times rather than the period to which it ostensibly refers. If so, Acts 14^{23} and 20^{17} reflect a system where the leadership is in the hands of a council of elders, and there is no reference to a figure corresponding to the bishop of I Timothy. This looks close to the situation reflected in Tit. 1^5 – even the wording is similar enough to raise the question of a relationship between the two writings. I Clement 42 uses the same titles as I Timothy – 'bishops and deacons', a combination which made its first appearance in Paul's own lifetime (Phil. 1^1). In both these cases, it is more likely that a group of leaders, here called 'bishops', elsewhere 'elders', is in mind rather than a single episcopal figure.

We are closer to the picture in I Timothy and to what eventually became the general practice in the Church, when we turn to the letters of Ignatius of Antioch. In those writings we can see both a structure and a concept of the work which are close to those in our present passage. And it is instructive to see the situation from the other side – that is, from the standpoint of the man actually exercising the office of bishop. As in the case of 'Timothy', the bishop may be a young man and must not be despised on that account (Mag. 3, cf. ECW, p. 87; I Tim. 4^{12}). In both writers, bishop and deacons are closely associated. Ignatius is undoubtedly the distinct leader of his church – and does all he can to safeguard and promote the same system in the churches to which he writes. But in two leading respects he goes further than our writer. First, for him the episcopal office is more strongly charismatic: he exercises wonderful powers of inspired speech, e.g. Philad. 7, cf. ECW, p. 113. And, closely related

* See A. E. Harvey, 'Elders', JTS, 25, 1974, p. 318ff.; and C. H. Roberts, Elders: a Note', JTS, 26, 1975, pp. 403ff.
† cf. J. L. Houlden, The Johannine Epistles, A. & C. Black, 1974, p. 4.

to this, his role is deeply mysterious, springing from the very heart of the revelation to which he bears witness. Ignatius never tires of affirming that the bishop is the very image of God himself (just as the deacons are, usually, the image of Jesus): e.g. Mag. 6; Smyrn. 8; Trall 3. So, his authority derives from this source and is authenticated by God alone (Philad. 1). Unlike our writer, he feels no need to lean on the posthumous authority of Paul or any other human figure. In that respect, Ignatius is closer to the Paul of history who acknowledged only the call of God as the basis for his position.

In both Ignatius and I Timothy, it is opposition which leads to the stress on constituted authority. I Timothy opens with an attack on erroneous teaching of Gnostic type. Though chapter 3 does not return to the theme, the officers of the community are part of the orderly system which our writer puts forward as the antidote to false teaching and undesirable behaviour. Perhaps the list of moral qualities given here was already conventional – formulated independently of the immediate circumstances which provoke the writing of the Epistle. Other passages, I Tim. 4[11ff.] and Tit. 1[9ff.], refer to the duty of teaching true doctrine. In Ignatius, the tone is more strident (he protests, we might think, a little too much about the dignity of his office), and there is certainly a stronger theological sense: he is much more explicit about the positions to be opposed (e.g on the reality of the incarnation, Rom. 7, cf. *ECW*, p. 77; Eph. 18–20, cf. *ECW*, p. 81; on the centrality of the Eucharist, Philad. 4, cf. *ECW*, p. 112)* and is not content with a rather general defence of orthodoxy, such as we find here.

I

The saying is sure: cf. 1[15], p. 59f. It is possible that as in 4[9] and Tit. 3[8] the reference is to the preceding not the following statement. If, as is likely (cf. p. 72), the salvation referred to in 2[15] is that of the life to come or the coming age, then this view is confirmed; for that is the subject of all the other sayings (except perhaps 1[15]) to which this statement is attached, and two of the others also use the verb 'save' (1[15] and Tit. 3[5]). However important Church order is for this writer and how-

*On all these questions, see H. von Campenhausen, *Ecclesiastical Authority and Spiritual Power in the Church of the First Three Centuries*, A. & C. Black 1969, especially chapter V.

ever practical and down to earth he often shows himself to be, it is unlikely that the saying about the worthiness of ecclesiastical office would
qualify as a 'faithful saying'. It may even be an appropriate popular
saying taken over by the writer: the Greek has the abstract noun related
to *episkopos* (*bishop*) – 'To aspire to leadership is an honourable ambition'
(NEB). And some manuscripts have instead of *sure* (*pistos*), as in the
usual formula, the adjective *anthrōpinos* (= 'commonly accepted').
This reading has in its favour the fact that scribes would be strongly
impelled to change it to the commoner phrase rather than the reverse.
If it is the true reading, then the reference may well be to the following
rather than the preceding statement.

bishop: episkopos, 'overseer', is used in Greek in both secular and religious contexts, and thence enters Christian usage. The more Jewish
term is *elder*. In these writings (cf. 5^{17} and Tit. 1$^{5ff.}$, see p. 142) the titles
overlap, with 'elder' perhaps relating more to status, 'bishop' more to
function. It is likely that at least in many churches an original body of
elders eventually gave rise to the concentration of leadership in the
hands of a single bishop. Linguistic evidence and the sparse historical
material at our disposal point to this, but it is quite impossible to be
sure. In some places, 'elder' seems to have been the title for the single,
ruling figure, cf. II John ^{1}.

2ff.
The list of virtues, much of it repeated for the deacons in v. 8ff., contains few surprises. It is conventional in type, paralleled in numerous
Jewish, pagan and Christian sources. For close parallels, cf. Tit. 1$^{6ff.}$;
Polycarp, Philippians 5ff. (cf. *ECW*, p. 146); Gal. 5^{22}; Col. 3$^{12ff.}$; and
in the Dead Sea Scrolls, The Community Rule 4. The make-up of the
list represents our writer's values. As far as most of its elements are
concerned (but see v. 6), it is hard to see how these characteristics differ
from what is desirable in all Christians (to whom in Paul such lists
always apply). Is there here perhaps a sign of incipient clericalism?
Already special and higher standards are expected of office-holders in
the Church than of ordinary lay members. If there is a suggestion of
this here, it is the fount of a long tradition.

the husband of one wife: polygamy was known in Judaism, but is unlikely
to be in mind here. It is hard to believe it was left as even implicitly
permissible to non-office-holding Christians of these Hellenistic Churches. So it is not surprising that other senses are sought. It might mean
that second marriage after the death of the first partner is forbidden.

But in the case of young widows this is positively encouraged, 5¹⁴, and it is hard to see why, if no deep principle were involved, such a prohibition should apply only to Church officers. So perhaps a third possibility is the most likely: 'faithful to his own wife' (NEB). It is simply an enjoining of marital fidelity, and, like other qualities in the list, presumably it applied in effect to all Christians. If this is the sense, the oddity of the expression is not relieved by the fact that it is repeated in v. 12 and Tit. 1⁶; cf. I Tim. 5⁹, p. 93, which confirms our interpretation.

dignified: kosmios, the adjective cognate with the words translated *adorn* and *seemly* in 2⁹.

hospitable: this virtue was much prized in early Christianity, often because of the needs of travelling Christian messengers, probably the chief means of contact between congregations which still, and for some time to come, had little in the way of organization to bind them together; cf. II John¹⁰; III John; Didache 11f., cf. *ECW*, pp. 232ff. This aspect of early Church life does not, however, figure explicitly in these writings; cf. Tit. 1⁸.

apt teacher: cf. 5¹⁷; probably already a special duty of the *episkopos*. As time went on it became his chief role – the guardian of orthodoxy.

3f
no lover of money: a leading theme of early Christian moral exhortation, especially prominent in Luke-Acts and James.* Sometimes it springs straight from the heart of Christian faith, cf. II Cor. 8⁹; sometimes it probably reflects the social status of many of the first Christians; here, it seems rather to be part of a rounded picture of the temperate man.

respectful: cf. 2².

5
own household ... God's church: the idea that household management is the starting-point and model for wider responsibilities is a commonplace of Greek thought; for its classical exposition, see Aristotle's *Politics.* It is typical of the ideal of general, secular respectability which is outlined in this passage. It may also reflect the fact that the earliest

*cf. J. L. Houlden, *Ethics and the New Testament*, Penguin, 1973, pp. 57ff, 88ff.

Christian congregations centred on households (cf. Col. 4¹⁵), and developed much of their morality from contemporary codes of household ethics (e.g. Col. 3¹⁸ff.). Here, the process of growth from 'household' to 'congregation' has gone some way (cf. in 5⁴).

6f.

not a recent convert: this does not of itself imply a post-Pauline date for this work, but it points towards it. Once more, it sees office depending not so much on charismatic gifts or insistent divine call (cf. Paul himself, Gal. 1) as on solid qualifications. However, the stated reason for the bishop's not being a neophyte (*neophutos*, lit. 'newly planted' – this is its first attested use in the derived sense) is the danger to his own character; as we have seen, modesty ranks high in our writer's scale of virtues.

the devil: this is almost certainly the right translation. The margin suggests the more fundamental meaning of the word *diabolos* because it is used in that sense in v. 11. However, the definite article makes it unlikely (cf. also II Tim. 2²⁶).

condemnation ... snare: either that into which the devil had already fallen or that into which he traps others. More probably the latter, in view of the thought expressed in the closing verses of ch. 2 (cf. also 6⁹).

8ff.

deacons: diakonos, lit. 'servant'. The word acquires technical meaning only in Christianity. As we have seen, it is uncertain how far that stage has already been reached here. Clearly, there is already movement towards it (v. 13). There is no mention here of derivation from the role of Jesus himself, as Mk. 10⁴⁵ might imply and as the letters of Ignatius never tire of stating (e.g. Magn. 6, cf. *ECW*, p. 88; Trall. 3, cf. *ECW*, p. 95). As far as we can tell, our writer sees the diaconate simply as an office in the Church, part of the accepted structure.

It is perhaps not surprising that the list of qualifications is close to that just given for bishops. It has led some to question whether it is not anachronistic to see here much difference between the status of the two groups. That may be the situation in Phil. 1¹, which is considerably earlier, and indeed there the two may be alternative titles for the same persons. But here the bishop's role is sufficiently distinctive, above all in the realm of teaching and preaching. Indeed, a difficulty lies in the absence of any definition of the deacons' work. Later their particular

THE FIRST LETTER TO TIMOTHY

duties lay in the sphere of care of the Church's money and goods, to-gether with the relief of the poor of the congregation. It is possible that the story in Acts 6 (which has the verb 'serve' but not the title) represents a reading back into the Church's early days of this role, current for a group of Church officers in the writer's time. Ignatius speaks of the deacons' place in the liturgical gatherings of the Church. Our writer assumes that his readers know what deacons do. Only the hint that, like the bishops, they are not to be *greedy for gain* (v. 8) implies that an important part of the work of both groups was seen as the management of the congregation's business affairs. Whatever took up the greater part of their time, there is no doubt that the teaching func-tion dominates at least the bishop's life in the view of our writer.

mystery: the word adds nothing to the simple expression *the faith,* which is the writer's common usage. It has a richer sense in Paul, re-ferring to the esoteric nature of the Gospel (or parts of it) which has now been disclosed by God's act in Christ, cf. I Cor. 2^7; 15^{51}; Col. $1^{25f.}$. There is here none of that esoteric feeling, which Paul shared with many others in the ancient world (the word has the same sonority in pagan and Jewish usage e.g. the Dead Sea Scrolls, cf. Vermes, p. 189); cf. v. 16.

11

the women: discussion of deacons is resumed in v. 12, so the reference is most probably to their wives. Or else to deaconesses (cf. Rom. 16^1); but our writer seems to see widows as the women's group in the official structure of the community ($5^{3ff.}$), so the first suggestion stands.

13

standing ... confidence: both these words could have spiritual signifi-cance. The former can refer in the language of Gnosticism to rank in the progress of the soul towards heaven. The latter frequently in early Christian usage refers to the boldness which the believer is given before God and will exercise in particular on the Last Day (e.g. Eph. 3^{12}; I John 2^{28}). It is not uncharacteristic that here the sense is almost certainly this-worldly. The subject is reputation and assurance in the context of Church life here and now.

80

[14] *I hope to come to you soon, but I am writing these instructions to you so that,* [15] *if I am delayed, you may know how one ought to behave in the household of God, the pillar and bulwark of the truth.* [16] *Great indeed, we confess, is the mystery of our religion:*

> *He[f] was manifested in the flesh,*
> *vindicated[g] in the Spirit,*
> *seen by angels,*
> *preached among the nations,*
> *believed on in the world,*
> *taken up in glory.*

4 [1] *Now the Spirit expressly says that in later times some will depart from the faith by giving heed to deceitful spirits and doctrines of demons,* [2] *through the pretensions of liars whose consciences are seared,* [3] *who forbid marriage and enjoin abstinence from foods which God created to be received with thanksgiving by those who believe and know the truth.* [4] *For everything created by God is good, and nothing is to be rejected if it is received with thanksgiving;* [5] *for then it is consecrated by the word of God and prayer.*

[6] *If you put these instructions before the brethren, you will be a good minister of Christ Jesus, nourished on the words of the faith and of the good doctrine which you have followed.* [7] *Have nothing to do with godless and silly myths. Train yourself in godliness;* [8] *for while bodily training is of some value, godliness is of value in every way, as it holds promise for the present life and also for the life to come.* [9] *The saying is sure and worthy of full acceptance.* [10] *For to this end we toil and strive,[h] because we have our hope set on the living God, who is the Saviour of all men, especially of those who believe.*

[11] *Command and teach these things.* [12] *Let no one despise your youth, but set the believers an example in speech and conduct, in love, in faith, in purity.* [13] *Till I come, attend to the public reading of scripture, to preaching, to teaching.* [14] *Do not neglect the gift you have, which was given you by prophetic utterance when the elders laid their hands upon you.* [15] *Practise these duties, devote yourself to them, so that all may see your progress.* [16] *Take heed to yourself and to your teaching; hold to that, for by so doing you will save both yourself and your hearers.*

[f]Greek *Who*; other ancient authorities read *God*; others, *Which*
[g]Or *justified*   [h]Other ancient authorities read *suffer reproach*

This passage raises no new major issues. It reinforces at many points
the picture already gained of the writer's mind. Precisely because it
adds so little, it shows what most deeply moves him: the importance
of the teaching of true doctrine by accredited leaders and the need to
eradicate false and foolish ideas. At certain points the nature of these
ideas becomes a little clearer, but they remain somewhat hazy, as
does the structure of the true doctrine. The placing side by side of a
fine and rich doctrinal formula (3^{16}) and teaching on the matter of
ascetic attitudes to marriage and food shows how uninterested our
writer is in sustained theological statement. Under the overriding
pressure to maintain the tradition, he moves without hesitation from
one level to another, one topic to another.

14f.
I hope to come etc.: this is another note designed to give Pauline verisimilitude. Labour spent on trying to square it with other information
about Paul's movements is wasted. It is included because it is typical,
cf. Rom. 1^{11}; 15^{24}; II Cor. 12^{14}; 13^1. As the sentence continues, it also
establishes the nature of the Pauline tradition: Paul's absence (and death)
is no obstacle to the continuance of his authority.

the household of God: it is uncertain how far this was still a lively image.
The idea of Israel as God's household ('the house of Israel', *oikos*, our
word) is an Old Testament commonplace, and Hellenistic paganism
used the expression for religious groups. The image is exploited in
Heb. 3^{2-6}, using its Old Testament background, cf. also I Peter 2^5; 4^{17}.
Often in the LXX, 'the Lord's house' is the Jerusalem temple: that
image had been applied to the Church by Paul: I Cor. 3^{16}; II Cor. 6^{16};
cf. Eph. $2^{19\text{ff.}}$. It may be in mind here, especially in view of the last
phrase of v. 15 (see below). But perhaps the more domestic image is
uppermost. The idea appeared in v. 4. And the extended treatment
given in these Epistles to the duties incumbent upon various groups of
people in the Church (cf. also Tit. $1^{6\text{ff.}}$; $2^{2\text{ff.}}$) seems to be modelled,
sometimes closely, on formulations popular in Jewish and pagan circles
at the time, stating the proper behaviour of husbands, wives, children,
slaves and other sections of families in society (cf. e.g. Col. $3^{18\text{ff.}}$). It

was not so long, after all, since the Christian congregations had been primarily domestic in their structure and basis, cf. Col. 4^{15}; Philemon 1$^{1f.}$. Even if, in certain respects, a more elaborate organization was now emerging, there is no doubt that the houses of members of the Church remained for at least another century the normal meeting places of the congregations.*

church: already Paul's word for the Christian community. It is used to some degree in the LXX for the congregation of Israel, and in secular Greek for an assembly, especially the meeting of citizens in a Greek city. Christians may have adopted it because an alternative, *sunagōgē*, had been taken by Hellenistic Judaism. It seems to have signified first the local congregation, especially when gathered for worship (Gal. 1^{22}; I Cor. 14^{19,34}), then the Church at large (I Cor. 12^{28}; Col. 1^{18,24}). Here, while the congregation is immediately in view, it looks as if the perspective naturally broadens to embrace the Church as a whole.

pillar: in Gal. 2^9, Paul uses the word, perhaps sarcastically, for the early apostles. I Clem. 5 (*ECW*, p. 25) does the same. Here it applies to the Church. cf. Eccles. 36^{24} for this general use of the image.

bulwark: *hedraiōma* here appears for the first time in extant Greek literature. The root meaning is 'support' and it is likely that 'foundation' would be the best translation. The Qumran *Community Rule* speaks of the members laying 'a foundation of truth for Israel, for the Community of the everlasting Covenant' (Vermes, p. 78). The word may be a symptom that we have here one example of that comparison between the Jewish Temple and the Christian dispensation which, with many variations, was so pervasive in early Christian thought (cf. e.g. John 2^{21}; Rev. 21^{22}). It has been suggested that in particular there lies behind the verse a Christian exegesis of I Kings 8$^{10-23}$, a passage using a similar range of ideas.†

16

we confess: A. T. Hanson has made out a good case for translating the adverb represented by these words (*homologoumenōs*) 'demonstrably'.‡ It is a word used in academic argument, and our writer may have

---

*cf. H. Chadwick, *The Early Church*, Penguin, 1967, p. 279.

†See B. Gärtner, *The Temple and the Community*, Cambridge University Press, 1965, pp. 66–71; A. T. Hanson, op. cit., ch. I.

‡op. cit., ch. 2.

picked it up from IV Maccabees, where, alone in the LXX, it occurs three times, always in relation to important statements. The work dates from perhaps a few decades before the Pastoral Epistles, and we have already (cf. p. 59) found one other point of contact: it is IV Maccabees which contains the greater number of LXX occurrences of *eusebeia*, which with its cognates is a key word of these writings (and not found much elsewhere in early Christian books) – and it appears in this sentence (translated *religion*). An academic flourish of this kind is out of character with our writer and a little pretentious. That he uses it here may help us to assess the formula which occupies the rest of the verse. On any showing, it is theologically more advanced and more speculative in character than these writings in general. The use of this adverb may indicate that the writer feels self-conscious in quoting such material: he is stretching beyond his normal reach.

the mystery of our religion: cf. on v. 9. But *mystery* has a little more force here. No doubt used because it was a Pauline word, its sonority again helps to introduce suitably the formula which follows.

This clause as a whole may be read not only as introducing the six-line statement of faith, but rather as an exclamation commenting enthusiastically on the preceding words about the Church. The Christian institution (not too strong a word), seen as the great support of true doctrine, is the key to a feeling of warm assurance about *our religion*. This last word seems to be used in a somewhat more concrete sense here than elsewhere: not so much 'piety' as the system of belief and practice which gives it shape. It is the same solidifying tendency as we find in this writer's use of 'faith' (cf. p. 48).

He was: the formula opens with a textual difficulty. Some manuscripts have 'God', which, while not impossible in view of the affiliations of this piece (see below), is both inadequately supported in the manuscripts and on balance unlikely – the statement concerns Christ. And surely, even in a formula, this writer could not have called Christ simply 'God'? It would seem wholly improbable (cf. 2⁵) if it were not for Tit. 2¹³, see the discussion on p. 150. The reading 'Which' is also unlikely to be original: it will have arisen to make the pronoun (*ho*) agree with *mystery*. The literal translation of the best text is 'Who' (a mere stroke would alter the Greek *hos* into the abbreviation for *theos*, 'God'). This awkward introduction points to our having here an extract from a longer formula of early Christian hymnody or prayer (it is certainly rhythmical and balanced). That means that it is impossible to comment usefully on the scope of the piece: it may be, for example, that the full statement contained reference to the death of Jesus, which, oddly it seems at first sight, is lacking here. With that caution, however, we can see pattern in these lines. They speak of Christ, not by taking us in order through the great saving acts of his death, burial and resurrections (cf. Acts 2$^{23f.}$; 4^{10}; I Cor. 15$^{3ff.}$), but by presenting him at the two contrasting and complementary levels of 'flesh' and 'spirit', heaven and earth. This perspective can be seen also in a passage (again probably liturgical in nature) like Phil. 2$^{6-11}$, where it is combined with the following of the historical order of Christ's career. Here we move repeatedly from the one level to the other. Taking 'earth' as A and 'heaven' as B, it runs: ABBAAB (see below for detailed exposition). (This chiastic structure is typically Jewish.) A passage which, though much simpler in structure, similarly thinks in terms of the two levels, flesh and spirit, is Rom. 1$^{3f.}$, where the presence of an already existing formula may again be suspected (cf. also I Peter 3^{18}).

The form of these lines is more regular than that of any of the comparable New Testament passages: each line consists of a passive verb in the aorist tense followed by *in* (except in line 3, where it is inappropriate) and a noun in the dative. Given the contemporary picture of the universe, in which the heavenly realms were thought of quite spatially, all the nouns represent 'places' (though wider considerations come into the meaning of *flesh* and *spirit* in lines 1 and 2).

The theology of the piece is surely not quite in our writer's most natural idiom: we have suggested that he himself was conscious of the fact. In tone, it surely comes close to what he might have condemned as myths and speculations (1^4). Not only does at least this part of the formula contain no reference to the death of Christ; its whole assumption is that he was an already existing spiritual being who at a certain point entered this world of matter only to triumph over it and resume heavenly status. There is here nothing like the stress on the reality of his involvement with the human lot which we find in the partly similar passage, Phil. 2$^{6-11}$. Only the aorist verbs bring in that element of 'event' which is so prominent in the general New Testament account of the work of Jesus. We may contrast the emphasis on *the man, Christ Jesus* in 2^5. Moreover, five out of the six lines deal with the triumph of Christ and its effects. Was this in fact where our writer would, out of choice, have placed the weight?

The other surprising feature of the passage, again in the light of the wide sweep of New Testament teaching, is the lack of any sense of the End. There is no hint of eschatology. It cannot be said that our writer was strong in his sense of the coming great Day, but he does not abandon it altogether (cf. II Tim. 4^8; Tit. 2^{13}). It is a sign that the kind of theology implicit in this passage finds its parallels in circles quite other than those represented by the rather prosaic and certainly unspeculative writer of the Pastoral Epistles. The writer of at least the greater part of the Gospel of John would have found it not uncongenial.* So, with regard to the wide cosmic sweep of the passage, would Ignatius of Antioch, whose other links with our writer are in the area of Church organization rather than theology: see e.g. Eph. 19 (*ECW*, p. 81), where the reference to God appearing in human form compares with the variant reading here (see above). Ignatius, however, also emphasizes strongly the death of Jesus and the reality of his humanity.†

manifested: the word appears again in a similar sense in II Tim. 1[10], but in the New Testament it is chiefly a Pauline and, closer to our present use of it, Johannine word: cf. I John 1[2]; 3[5].

flesh . . . *Spirit:* apart from signifying two contrasting spheres of existence, these terms probably carry the sense of two rival powers under which man may live. In that case, the capital S is justified. Jesus made an appearance within the realm of flesh (many Christians in the coming decades were to stress that it was no more than merely an appearance), but his triumph was firmly in the realm dominated by divine spirit and made possible by its power.

vindicated: in Paul, this word is technical, 'justified' (*dikaioō*). Here it has a simpler sense, referring to Christ's victory over evil powers by the strength of God. cf. Col. 2[15].

seen by angels: the verb (*ōphthē*) is almost a technical term for heavenly manifestations, cf. I Cor. 15[5]. The reference here is probably to the angels who greeted Christ on his heavenward journey after his resurrection, a common feature of early Christian belief but nowhere explicitly described in the New Testament itself. It is implicit however in Phil. 2[10].‡ Just as flesh–spirit and world–glory form pairs, so also do angels–nations. They are contrasted as heavenly and earthly, but also

---

* See E. Käsemann, *The Testament of Jesus*, SCM, 1966.

† See E. Schweizer in W. Klassen and G. F. Snyder (eds.), *Current Issues in New Testament Interpretation*, SCM, 1962, ch. 10; R. H. Gundry in W. W. Gasque and R. P. Martin (eds.), *Apostolic History and the Gospel*, Paternoster Press, 1970, pp. 203–22; J. D. G. Dunn, 'Jesus – Flesh and Spirit', *JTS*, 24, 1973, p. 62ff.

‡ For the more developed story, cf. Justin, First Apology, ch. 51, *LCC*, I, p. 275.

linked by the belief that the heavenly powers governed the earthly.
The yielding of allegiance to Christ by the former was the prelude to
the submission of the latter.

4,1

the Spirit expressly says: an allusion to the common theme of apocalyptic
prophecy that the End would be preceded by suffering and catastrophe
and the apostasy of many of God's people. (So *husteros* should probably
be taken as 'last' rather than *later*, though *eschatos* is commoner.) See,
for example, Dan. $12^{1f.}$; Mark 13^{14-22}; Rev. 13^{5-10}. Perhaps Jewish or
Christian written apocalypses, seen as inspired, are in mind; perhaps
charismatic preaching.

doctrines of demons: Paul and the author of I John also saw diabolical
agents at work in the teaching which they opposed, cf. II Cor. 4^4; I
John 2^{18}; cf. John 13^2.

3f.

forbid marriage: the depreciation of the material and the physical which
was a leading mark of Gnostics and the like issued sometimes in liber-
tinism, sometimes in extreme asceticism. Contempt could lead in
either direction. Both paths were inimical to traditional Jewish piety
and so to those Christians who inherited much of its outlook. It is
asceticism of this brand which is under fire here. Though these views
characterized Gnostics of the second century and would have been rejected by traditional Judaism (Jewish abstinence from certain foods was
motivated simply by obedience to the Law not by ascetic principle),
we can by no means assume that Jewish opponents are not in mind here.
Our pseudonymous writer may possibly not have a precise picture but
simply be stating a case against all enemies of the faith; yet it seems
certain that some Jews of this period took up the positions he is opposing: cf. Col. $2^{21f.}$; and on I Tim. 1^4, p. 56; Tit. $1^{10,14}$.*
   Paul, partly because he shared to some degree the cast of mind which
came to its height in Gnosticism but more because of his conviction
that the End was near, took a moderately negative view of marriage,
cf. I Cor. 7,† but, for different reasons, partly relating to his belief
about the Jewish Law, a liberal position on food taboos (I Cor. 8 and
10). He was not motivated, in other words, by simple arguments con-

*For asceticism at Qumran, see M. Black, *The Scrolls and Christian Origins*,
Nelson, 1961, p. 27ff.
†See J. C. Hurd, *The Origins of I Corinthians*, SPCK, 1965.

cerned with asceticism but by more fundamental theological factors. Our writer works at the more superficial level and takes the non-ascetic view.

So he finds himself differing from a plain reading of Paul on marriage but agreeing with him on food. He shows, by his attitude on the latter issue, that his piety has developed beyond that of Judaism under the influence of Christian tradition. Not that he lacks a certain asceticism of his own. If he has no wish to forbid marriage, at least he will regulate it in some cases, as 5[9ff.] shows. Typically, his asceticism appears in institutional guise. And v. 8 makes a common-sense estimate. For Paul's teaching on asceticism, cf. Col. 2[20-23]. For *thanksgiving*, cf. I Cor. 10[30]; also Rom. 14[6].

5

the word of God: probably, in view of the allusions to the Creation in v. 3f., the word by which God created the world, cf. Ps. 33[6]; Wisdom of Solomon 9[1]; John 1[1-3]. Or perhaps it duplicates *prayer* – the grace which is said over food.

6

minister: the same word as *deacon* (3[8]), *diakonos*, here used in its general sense, 'servant', in a phrase virtually taken from Paul, II Cor. 11[23]; Col. 1[7].

7

myths: cf. 1[4], p. 55.

godliness: i.e. religion as our writer sees it. Equivalent to 'the faith', or rather to its expression in prayer and life.

8

bodily training: we may have here a popular saying. In any case, it refers back to the views attacked in v. 3. Observance of the true faith pays assured and ample dividends. Perhaps the whole of v. 8 was a favourite item in our writer's repertory; so v. 9 may imply (see p. 59f. Also cf. p. 107).

10

strive: almost certainly the better reading, for it continues the athletic metaphor; but some manuscripts have *suffer reproach*, an alteration made perhaps in times of persecution.

Saviour: cf. p. 47.

all men, especially etc.: cf. 2^4. Realism alongside idealism. Or else we may see it as a liberal doctrine within the accepted gamut of eschatological speculation (contrast Rev. 20^{15}). The one God (cf. 2^5, p. 67) is Lord of all mankind and is the Saviour (*for* rather than *of* probably represents the writer's real intention) all; nevertheless his faithful people will take the lead. More cautious than Paul's I Cor. 15^{22} and Rom. $11^{25\text{ff.}}$.

11
teach: cf. p. 55.

12
your youth: cf. p. 74f.

13f.
See p. 75.

laid their hands: cf. 5^{22}; II Tim. 1^6. This action was used for many purposes in the world of the early Church. In the New Testament, it is done for blessing (Mk. 10^{16}), for commissioning missionaries (Acts 13^3), for conveying the Spirit to new converts (Acts 8^{17}), and, here, for ordaining new officers of the congregation. Rabbis were ordained by the same act. The common factor is the passing on of power for a special function or purpose. Generally, the activity of the Spirit is closely associated with the act. Here it operates through inspired designation of the men concerned (cf. 1^{18}), perhaps by existing leaders or by specially trusted speakers recognized as channels of God's choice. The agents entitled to lay hands for this purpose cannot have been closely defined: here it is the elders, in 5^{22} it is 'Timothy', in II Tim. 1^6 the apostle. But in this latter passage the emphasis is perhaps less on ordination to office than on the handing on of authentic tradition (*via* the fictitious setting of the letter); while in 5^{22} discipline seems to be the subject. The act, even for this writer, had several nuances.

elders: See pp. 74, 92, 142.

5¹–6²ᵃ   RULES FOR WIDOWS AND OTHERS

1 Do not rebuke an older man but exhort him as you would a father; treat younger men like brothers, 2 older women like mothers, younger women like sisters, in all purity.

3 Honour widows who are real widows. 4 If a widow has children or grandchildren, let them first learn their religious duty to their own family and make some return to their parents; for this is acceptable in the sight of God. 5 She who is a real widow, and is left all alone, has set her hope on God and continues in supplications and prayers night and day; 6 whereas she who is self-indulgent is dead even while she lives. 7 Command this, so that they may be without reproach. 8 If any one does not provide for his relatives, and especially for his own family, he has disowned the faith and is worse than an unbeliever.

9 Let a widow be enrolled if she is not less than sixty years of age, having been the wife of one husband; 10 and she must be well attested for her good deeds, as one who has brought up children, shown hospitality, washed the feet of the saints, relieved the afflicted, and devoted herself to doing good in every way. 11 But refuse to enrol younger widows; for when they grow wanton against Christ they desire to marry, 12 and so they incur condemnation for having violated their first pledge. 13 Besides that, they learn to be idlers, gadding about from house to house, and not only idlers but gossips and busybodies, saying what they should not. 14 So I would have younger widows marry, bear children, rule their households, and give the enemy no occasion to revile us. 15 For some have already strayed after Satan. 16 If any believing woman¹ has relatives who are widows, let her assist them; let the church not be burdened, so that it may assist those who are real widows.

17 Let the elders who rule well be considered worthy of double honour, especially those who labour in preaching and teaching; 18 for the scripture says, 'You shall not muzzle an ox when it is treading out the grain', and, 'The labourer deserves his wages'. 19 Never admit any charge against an elder except on the evidence of two or three witnesses. 20 As for those who persist in sin, rebuke them in the presence of all, so that the rest may stand in fear. 21 In the presence of God and of Christ Jesus and of the elect angels I charge you to keep these rules without favour, doing nothing from partiality. 22 Do not be hasty in the laying on of hands, nor participate in another man's sins; keep yourself pure.

²³ No longer drink only water, but use a little wine for the sake of your stomach and your frequent ailments.

²⁴ The sins of some men are conspicuous, pointing to judgment, but the sins of others appear later. ²⁵ So also good deeds are conspicuous; and even when they are not, they cannot remain hidden.

6 ¹ Let all who are under the yoke of slavery regard their masters as worthy of all honour, so that the name of God and the teaching may not be defamed. ² Those who have believing masters must not be disrespectful on the ground that they are brethren; rather they must serve all the better since those who benefit by their service are believers and beloved.

¹Other ancient authorities read *man or woman*; others, simply *man*.

How do these extensive rules for the administration of widows contribute to the picture of Church life which we build up from these writings? The most notable feature is the degree of detail, far greater than for the bishop, for deacons, elders or slaves, the other categories dealt with in this letter. While clearly the officers of the congregation are already surrounded with a considerable degree of formality, it is small compared with the Christian widows.

In making our assessment, we ought not to let ourselves be influenced by the more recent significance of parts of these writings. Since the Reformation and particularly in negotiations for reunion between churches of Catholic and Protestant tradition, I Timothy has played an important role in providing scriptural precedent for this or that system of Church order – a major difficulty being that it is susceptible of more than one interpretation when set in the light of later institutions. In such discussion, attention has concentrated chiefly on the material concerning bishops and elders. But if we take the work at its face value, the widows are at least as significant a group. Perhaps the reason is that they were more troublesome than any other group. They needed more careful regulation. But on any showing they were a prominent element in the congregation (or congregations) with which our writer was concerned.

In that respect he shows his faithfulness to Pauline precedent. The regulating is new, but the giving of importance in Church life to women is not. Their place was limited and defined (2⁸⁻¹⁵), but it was fully recognized. We may compare the role of Apphia (Philem. ²), Phoebe (Rom. 16¹), Prisca and Mary (Rom. 16³,⁶).

In Jewish and pagan works giving lists of duties for various groups in society, there is no parallel to this treatment of widows. The passage reflects not only the position of women in Christian congregations, but also the cohesion within the group and the responsibility shouldered by the community for its needy members – and in the ancient world, elderly widows without families to support them were among the most exposed sections of society.

1

an older man: in our writer's mind, there appears to be a blurring of the distinction between grades in the Church hierarchy and age-groups or social groups in the congregation. In the former category we can clearly place the bishop and the deacons (ch. 3), and in the latter the widows and slaves, as well as the groups listed in v. 2. But *presbuteros* may belong to both. Here it is translated *older man*, but it appears in v. 17 as *elder*, an official of the congregation. Both renderings are appropriate. No doubt the body of elders was made up of the senior members of the church. The ambiguity at this point illustrates a more general confusion. The widows themselves overlap a little on to the 'clerical' side: their duty is to pray, just as the bishop and the elders are to preach and teach. The same difficulty in assessing whether we are dealing with an institutional title or not at this early stage of the Church's life arises in relation to I John 2¹²⁻¹⁴, evidence from another congregation at about the same period. It seemed natural to our writer to mention duties towards the various groups to be found in any large family, alongside those which belong more specifically to the Church (like bishop, deacons and widows), an indication of the close relationship between much of the contents of this letter and the conventional compendiums of duties within households that were common in both pagan and Jewish circles (cf. p. 78f.).

younger men: cf. I John 2¹³ᶠ·, where it is possible that a more formal group within the congregation is intended.★

3

real widows: probably those who qualify under the conditions given in v. 5 and v. 9ff. Like older man/elder and servant/deacon, the word *chēra* was beginning to acquire a technical sense in this circle of Chris-

★ cf. J. L. Houlden, *The Johannine Epistles*, A. & C. Black, 1974, p. 70ff.

tians, and in v. 9ff, is used in that way. Acts 6^1 knows them as a distinguishable group. Other Asia Minor congregations had the same institution at about the same period: cf. Ignatius, Smyrn. 13, cf. *ECW*, p.
123; Polycarp 4, cf. *ECW*, p. 128: 'Take care that widows are not
neglected; next to the Lord, be yourself their guardian'; and Polycarp,
Phil. 4, cf. *ECW*, p. 145: 'Widows ... should make constant intercessions ... avoid any tale-bearing' (cf. v. 13). We have the same set of
features as in our present passage: charitable support, moral requirements and the duty of prayer (cf. p. 65). The 'order of widows' continued to be a common feature of Christian congregations in the following centuries.

4

their religious duty: the reference is to the fifth of the Ten Command-
ments, Ex. 20^{12}; cf. Eph. $6^{1ff.}$; Mark $7^{10ff.}$ (*them*, the *children or grandchildren*). The congregation is already sufficiently big and formally
organized to distinguish between its corporate responsibilities and the
individual duties of family groups within it.

5

night and day: cf. I Thess, 3^{10}.

8

disowned the faith: at this point family duty and Christian allegiance
merge. To break this fundamental law, inherited from Judaism (and
indeed enjoined in pagan ethics), is to betray one's Christianity, cf.
Mk. 7^{10-12}.

9

enrolled: an official word, used, for example, of soldiers. For the first
instances of charitable care of needy Christians, cf. Gal. 2^{10}; Acts 6^1.

wife of one husband: see on 3^2, p. 78. It is not that she must have been
married only once but that she must have been faithful during marriage.
v. 14 points to this interpretation.

10

hospitality: cf. 3^2, p. 78.

washed the feet of the saints: cf. John 13^{14}. Probably seen as an act of
religious devotion as well as of service. *The saints:* i.e. Christians, mem-

bers of God's people; the common New Testament sense, but only here in these writings.

11

wanton against Christ: seeds of the idea of Christian discipleship as marriage to Christ are to be found in I Cor. 6[16]; but though the image in that passage is powerful, it is not exploited in any hard or literal way. It may be that our writer's congregation, moving typically in this direction, has formalized the idea in creating a spirituality for its widows.

12

pledge: lit. 'faith' (*pistis*).

14

I would have: boulomai, as in 2[8], cf. p. 69. As throughout the Pastoral Epistles, order and stability are primary aims, in domestic as in Church life. Once more, the picture is quite different from the eschatological perspective apparent in Paul's discussion of family life in I Cor. 7 (but cf. Eph. 5[22ff.]).

the enemy: it is unclear whether human opponents or the devil are in mind; but cf. v. 15; and 3[6f]. The same word is used in II Thess. 2[4], where its application is again uncertain.

16

woman: the word is not in the text, but simply the adjective *pistē* ('faithful'). Some manuscripts have the masculine, instead or in addition, perhaps because it seemed more likely that men, as heads of households, would be in a position to take responsibility for widows in their families. Unless the 'faithful one' is herself meant to be a widow (and able to shoulder the care of others), this verse would fit better after v. 8.

17

elders: cf. 4[14] and Tit. 1[5]. The regulations given here are not comparable to those for the bishop and the deacons, in that they deal not with qualifications for office but with payment and discipline. This may support the view that 'the elders' were still simply 'the seniors' (cf. p. 74), i.e. the passage of time rather than any process of choice gave them their position (but cf. Tit. 1[5ff.]). Nevertheless, once they had gained it, they could be paid for it – again an indication of the degree of organization already attained. And they could be removed, after due process, if their behaviour warranted such a step.

The references to elders in the New Testament come from sources diverse enough to indicate that the title was common in a number of different parts of the Church by the end of the first century: see Acts 11^{30}; 14^{23}; 15^{6}; James 5^{14}; II John 1; III John 1; cf. also I Clem. 1 (note ambiguity again), 21, 44, cf. *ECW*; Ignatius, Trallians 2f. (*ECW*, p. 95f., which has the rendering 'clergy'). It is most natural to suppose that the title was derived from the usage of the Jewish synagogue, but the evidence for a period as early as this is surprisingly sparse, especially for Jews of the Dispersion. It is used for leaders of the people in wider senses in the LXX, and Luke 7^{3} attests its use for the leaders of a local Jewish community in Palestine at the time of Jesus.* Use of the term in Egypt for councils of various kinds cannot be said to throw much light on its adoption by the Church.

who rule well: perhaps the uncertainty whether 'elder-status' was simply recognized at a certain stage in a man's life or needed special qualifications (see above) is eased if we take it that only certain elders exercised active leadership. It is tempting to suppose that 'ruling' (or 'presiding') elders were the same as 'bishops' – were it not that 'Timothy' is probably seen in that position and is regarded as a young man (4^{11}), while elders were still surely elderly. In these respects the picture is unclear. We cannot be sure whether all elders rule but only some rule well, or only some rule at all. It is clear, however, that not all preach and teach: again, it is tempting to see a link with the episcopal office (cf. 3^{2}; 4^{13}).

double honour: almost certainly in view of v. 18, *timē* is being used in its sense of stipend (note our honorarium). (cf. Acts 28^{10}, only other New Testament use in its material sense.) Payment for Church work had been an issue for Paul. While he asserted his right to be paid, and appealed to the scriptural text (Deut. 25^{4}) used in v. 18, nevertheless he preferred to retain independence (I Cor. 9$^{9-14}$). Now, perhaps fifty years later, such a policy was not to be recommended for Church officers. Our writer may be counteracting the possibility of appealing to the passage in I Corinthians. The implication seems to be that non-ruling elders were paid at a certain rate, which was doubled in the case of those who presided (well).

* cf. *TDNT*, VI, p. 66ff.; and citations on p. 75.

18

'*you shall not muzzle*' etc.: the use of this text in this sense is a typical example of scribal exegetical method.

'*the labourer*' etc.: the saying appears in the same words in Luke 10⁷. It is noteworthy that our writer can call it by the technical term – *scripture* – normally reserved for the Old Testament in Christian usage of this period. It is just possible he applies it only to his first quotation. There is no acknowledgement of it as a saying of Jesus: perhaps it was a proverb.

19

two or three witnesses: the standard Jewish requirement, cf. Deut. 17⁶; 19¹⁵; also Matt. 18¹⁶, where the procedure is not specifically confined to leaders. For comparable methods at Qumran, see The Community Rule 8 (cf. Vermes, p. 85). V. 20 is probably linked to v. 19, concerning elders alone.

21

The solemnity of the statement is a measure of the writer's seriousness about maintaining the highest standards in the congregation. cf. II Tim. 4¹.

elect angels: probably, by distinction from fallen angels, cf. Jude ⁶. For the idea of Jesus with an escort of angels, cf. Mark 8³⁸; Luke 2¹³; Justin, First Apology, 6 (*LCC*, I, p. 245). For a very close parallel, cf. Luke 9²⁶.

22

The thought seems to be that if great care is taken in *either* reconciling offending elders *or* appointing them in the first place (cf. p. 142), trouble will be avoided. Which interpretation should be taken depends on whether v. 22 is to be linked with the verses immediately preceding it, or with the wider context of the whole passage on elders. The second remark, which continues the subject of exercising discipline, seeing it now from the responsible officer's side, inclines to the former view (cf. p. 94).

23

use wine: the officer aiming at purity (v. 22) may have been inclined to excessively temperate habits, cf. 3³; 4³ᶠ·. The medicinal motive nicely avoids facing the ascetic question head on.

24f.

The theme of discipline again. A group of purely general remarks rounds off the section.

6, 1f.

the yoke of slavery: with these verses, cf. Tit. 2$^{9f.}$; Col. 3$^{22ff.}$; Eph. 6$^{5ff.}$; I Peter 2$^{18ff.}$; also Philem. ^{16}. *All who* renders *hosoi*, lit. 'as many as': so the passage may refer to elders who are slaves. Relationships within the Christian community are to sweeten not sour those in general society. The *masters* in v. 1 are not Christians, by contrast with those in v. 2. As in the other New Testament passages on this theme, there is no question of disturbing the social system. Just as in the case of the relationship between the sexes our writer drops the Pauline doctrine which contains the seed of revolution (see on 2$^{8ff.}$, p. 65), so here the vital complement to Paul's conservative aspect is lacking: 'there is neither slave nor free ... you are all one in Christ Jesus' (Gal. 3^{28}). Once more, stability and the good name of the Church are the chief interests (cf. 3^{7}).

6^{2b-21} THE TRUE RELIGION

^{2b} *Teach and urge these duties.* ^{3} *If any one teaches otherwise and does not agree with the sound words of our Lord Jesus Christ and the teaching which accords with godliness,* ^{4} *he is puffed up with conceit, he knows nothing; he has a morbid craving for controversy and for disputes about words, which produce envy, dissension, slander, base suspicions,* ^{5} *and wrangling among men who are depraved in mind and bereft of the truth, imagining that godliness is a means of gain.* ^{6} *There is great gain in godliness with contentment;* ^{7} *for we brought nothing into the world, and^j we cannot take anything out of the world;* ^{8} *but if we have food and clothing, with these we shall be content.* ^{9} *But those who desire to be rich fall into temptation, into a snare, into many senseless and hurtful desires that plunge men into ruin and destruction.* ^{10} *For the love of money is the root of all evils; it is through this craving that some have wandered away from the faith and pierced their hearts with many pangs.*

^{11} *But as for you, man of God, shun all this; aim at righteousness, godliness, faith, love, steadfastness, gentleness.* ^{12} *Fight the good fight of the faith; take hold of the eternal life to which you were called when you made the good confession in the presence of many witnesses.* 13 *In the presence of God who gives life to all things, and of Christ Jesus who in his testimony before Pontius Pilate made the good confession,* 14 *I charge you to keep the commandment unstained and free from reproach until the appearing of our Lord Jesus Christ;* 15 *and this will be made manifest at the proper time by the blessed and only Sovereign, the King of kings and Lord of lords,* 16 *who alone has immortality and dwells in unapproachable light, whom no man has ever seen or can see. To him be honour and eternal dominion. Amen.*

17 *As for the rich in this world, charge them not to be haughty, nor to set their hopes on uncertain riches but on God who richly furnishes us with everything to enjoy.* 18 *They are to do good, to be rich in good deeds, liberal and generous,* 19 *thus laying up for themselves a good foundation for the future, so that they may take hold of the life which is life indeed.*

20 *O Timothy, guard what has been entrusted to you. Avoid the godless chatter and contradictions of what is falsely called knowledge,* 21 *for by professing it some have missed the mark as regards the faith. Grace be with you.*

ʲOther ancient authorities insert *it is certain that*

The pattern of I Timothy is a set of alternating stripes – first concerning heresy, then some aspect of Church order. We come now to the last section attacking false doctrine, seen especially in relation to its effects on conduct. This time the tone is more strongly hortatory. There is little that is really new, except attacks on wealth which fit only imperfectly with the rest of the material. This part of the Epistle is less well controlled than the rest: it has a miscellaneous quality. There is however no doubt of the strength of the writer's adherence to the causes for which he fights.

3

teaches otherwise: cf. 1³; and Gal. 1⁶ᶠ· which is the Pauline source of this motif. Whereas, however, in Paul it is the heart of the Gospel which is at stake, here it appears to be the moral and social duties just outlined.

sound words of our Lord: it is impossible to know whether the writer had a tradition of sayings of Jesus to support his teaching or whether he had nothing precise in mind. As we have seen, his only statement which also appears on the lips of Jesus in the Gospels is noted as coming from that source (5^{18}). In any case, *sound words* (or *teaching*) is a favourite expression of this writer's – six times, e.g. 1^{10} and II Tim. 1^{13}.*

4

controversy etc.: cf. 1^4. As this chapter shows as well as any part of his work, our writer prefers practical religion to anything approaching abstract theological discussion. He had not in this respect quite inherited the mantle of his master Paul. He may nevertheless have rightly discerned the challenges of his own times.

5

godliness is a means of gain: cf. Tit. 1^{11}. In view of 5$^{17f.}$, could not the heretics have levelled the same charge against the writer's party? The words serve to introduce the theme of greed for wealth and its recommended opposite, simplicity of life (v. 6–10).

6

contentment: or 'self-sufficiency'. A favourite virtue among the Stoics of the time (cf. Phil. 4^{11}). But perhaps here *autarkeia* has its simpler sense, 'sufficiency', 'a competence', as in II Cor. 9^8 (cf. v. 8 below).†

7

we brought nothing etc.: for this sentiment, cf. Job 1^{21}; Wis. of Sol. 7^6. See also v. 10.

10

for the love of money etc.: quoted as a popular saying. There are numerous instances in Greek literature. Polycarp also has it, in different wording (Phil. 4; cf. *ECW*, p. 145), then continues with words virtually identical with v. 7. cf. 3^3.

11

righteousness etc.: this impressive list of virtues is presented as the opposite of the love of money. Though out of this set only the words *pistis* and *agapē* (*faith* and *love*) appear in the comparable Pauline list in Gal. 5^{22}, we do find there words of similar sense (apart from *godliness*, which is not a Pauline virtue, cf. p. 59). But *pistis* here means probably something close to 'orthodoxy', while in Paul it is 'faithfulness'. And

*cf. also Philo, 'On Abraham', 223, F. H. Colson (ed.), *Philo*, VI, p. 109.
† See M. Hengel, *Property and Riches in the Early Church*, SCM, 1974, p. 57ff.

Paul's vices are commensurate with his virtues (cf. Gal. 5$^{19f.}$). *Righteousness:* simply 'uprightness'.

12–16
These verses (and probably v. 11), curiously intruded before the resumption of the theme of the wickedness of riches in v. 17, introduce a lofty and solemn tone. It has been suspected that they come from liturgical, perhaps in particular baptismal, use.

12
fight: the image is from the games rather than warfare (cf. 4^8; II Tim. 4^7; and I Cor. 9$^{24f.}$).

eternal life: all the other uses of this phrase in these writings refer to life after death or the life of the age to come after the return of Christ (1^{16}; Tit. 1^2; 3^7; see p. 6of.). It is likely that, expecting the End in the relatively near future, he does not clearly distinguish between the two. Here, however, we seem to have an example of the belief, which is at its strongest in the Johannine writings (e.g. John 3^{36}), that this 'life' is a present possession of the Christian: cf. also II Tim. 1^{10}. This is also the language of Paul, e.g. Rom. 6^{4,11}; 8^2.

the good confession: i.e. probably the profession of faith made in baptism. Despite the reference to the *many witnesses* again in II Tim. 2^2, where the occasion seems to be ordination, that is unlikely to be in mind here.

13
God who gives life: a common theme of theistic apologetic; cf. Acts 14^{15}; 17$^{24ff.}$. The verb *zōogoneō*, here and in Lk. 17^{33} and Acts 7^{19} only.

before Pontius Pilate: which Gospel account (if any) of the Passion of Jesus does the writer know? Mark depicts Jesus as virtually silent before Pilate (15$^{1-4}$), and both Matthew and Luke follow him. Only the Fourth Gospel shows Jesus stating his case at length to Pilate, and the account is written in such a way as hardly to bear comparison with the profession of faith in baptism. It is possible that the brief statements by Jesus in the synoptic Gospels' accounts (e.g. Mark 15^2, 'You have said so'), acknowledging the title 'King of the Jews', are sufficient to be compared with the confession of a candidate for baptism, as for example in the form 'Jesus is Lord' (Rom. 10^9; I Cor. 12^3). Or perhaps the writer knew a tradition concerning Jesus' trial which portrayed him more strongly than any of the Gospel accounts in the role of a martyr and contained a more ample statement of faith: our passage uses the word *testimony*, and this group of words (*martureō*) was speedily acquiring its technical sense concerned with martyrdom. Or else the reference is simply to Jesus' general demeanour: his act itself is a profession of faith. In any case, however, the connection between Christian baptism and the trial of Jesus as comparable events is somewhat strained. It lies only in the making of *the good confession*.

If these verses derive from a current formula used at baptisms, then we have here at least one of the roots of the reference to Pilate in the Apostles' Creed, which has its origin in baptismal use. Like that creed and the formulas which lie behind it, our passage has first a statement about God, then one about Jesus.

14

the commandment: probably the whole teaching which the writer enjoins.

the appearing: epiphaneia is one of the technical words for divine manifestation, used also in the imperial cult of the period. Apart from II Thess. 2^8 its use in the New Testament is confined to the Pastoral Epistles (cf. II Tim. 1^{10}; $4^{1,8}$; Tit. 2^{13}). In all cases except II Tim. 1^{10} it refers to the End, the return of Christ. *Parousia*, which lacks the wider associations, is the commoner New Testament term.

15

the proper time: or 'at his own time'. The event is assured but not necessarily imminent, as far as this writer is concerned. The matter is left in God's hands. We may contrast passages like Rom. 13^{12}; I Thess. 4^{13ff}.

Sovereign: dunastēs, 'a ruler'. For *only*, cf. 1^{17}.

King of kings and Lord of lords: cf. Rev. 17^{14}; 19^{16}. The first title is used of earthly rulers in Dan. 2^{37}; Ezek. 26^7; II Macc. 13^4. As titles for God. they appear in Jewish liturgical usage. cf. 1^{17}.

16

immortality: cf. 1^{17}. The flavour of the attributes of God given in this verse is that of Greek philosophy rather than the Jewish tradition, but the ideas have probably been mediated by the Hellenistic synagogue. God transcends the mortality of man and the visibility of matter. In the Old Testament, God's invisibility is spoken of (e.g. Ex. 33[20]); not, however, as a philosophical idea, but as an aspect of his 'otherness'.

To him etc.: the doxology is Jewish; cf. e.g. Heb. 13[21]; I Peter 4[11]; 5[11]. Two of these three parallels are similarly placed, i.e. towards the end of a letter. But in all three works, more follows. This was a recognized form.*

17
the rich: cf. vv. 6–10.   *to enjoy*: cf. 4[3f.].

19
laying up: cf. Matt. 6[20].

20
O Timothy: for this solemn final admonition, the supposed recipient, the representative of the tradition, comes once more into view.

what has been entrusted: lit., 'the deposit'. The image is financial. cf. II Tim. 1[12,14.].

contradictions: *antitheseis*. This was the title of the celebrated work by Marcion, the leading heretical teacher in the latter part of the first half of the second century. Some have seen here a cryptic reference to him. His teaching could well be designated *falsely called knowledge* (*gnōsis*); and as Paul was his great authority, it was clearly desirable for Christians of the central stream to recapture the apostle for their cause. What better way than pseudonymous writings of this kind, in which Paul is shown foreseeing and condemning the heretic? But one of Marcion's chief tenets was his rejection of Judaism; and the opponents attacked in these letters seem to be Jewish, even if their turn of mind could be described as Gnostic (cf. 1[7]; Tit. 1[14]). So unless our writer's attack is many-pronged (and at the expense of clarity), it is unlikely that there is any reference to Marcion. In any case, it would mean an improbably late date for the writing of these letters. Still, the anti-Marcion possibility lingers: it is possible that the reference to Jews in Tit. 1[14] is no more than 'scenery' to fill out the Pauline setting, and so may be discounted in the search for the writer's concerns (cf. p. 144). The commendation of the Old Testament scriptures in II Tim. 3[15f.] is consistent with opposition to Marcionite teachings. It is of course possible that this sentence

*cf. F. V. Filson, *Yesterday*, SCM, 1967, p. 22ff.

was inserted after the composition of the rest of I Timothy, extending its usefulness in a new direction and fully in line with its original nature and aim.

Grace be with you: a typical Pauline greeting concludes the work; cf. Col. 4^{18}; also Gal. 6^{18}; Phil. 4^{23}; I Thess. 5^{28}. *You* is plural, despite the singular address in 1^2. The same is true of the greetings which conclude the other two Pastoral Epistles.

The Second Letter to Timothy

TESTIMONY TO THE GOSPEL

¹ Paul, an apostle of Christ Jesus, by the will of God according to the promise of the life which is in Christ Jesus, ² to Timothy, my beloved child:
grace, mercy, and peace from God the Father and Christ Jesus our Lord.

³ I thank God whom I serve with a clear conscience, as did my fathers,
when I remember you constantly in my prayers. ⁴ As I remember your tears,
I long night and day to see you, that I may be filled with joy. ⁵ I am re-
minded of your sincere faith, a faith that dwelt first in your grandmother
Lois and your mother Eunice and now, I am sure, dwells in you. ⁶ Hence I
remind you to rekindle the gift of God that is within you through the laying
on of my hands; ⁷ for God did not give us a spirit of timidity but a spirit of
power and love and self-control.

⁸ Do not be ashamed then of testifying to our Lord, nor of me his
prisoner, but take your share of suffering for the gospel in the power of
God, ⁹ who saved us and called us with a holy calling, not in virtue of our
works but in virtue of his own purpose and the grace which he gave us in
Christ Jesus ages ago, ¹⁰ and now has manifested through the appearing of
our Saviour Christ Jesus, who abolished death and brought life and immortality to light through the gospel. ¹¹ For this gospel I was appointed a
preacher and apostle and teacher, ¹² and therefore I suffer as I do. But I am
not ashamed, for I know whom I have believed, and I am sure that he is
able to guard until that Day what has been entrusted to me.ᵃ ¹³ Follow the
pattern of the sound words which you have heard from me, in the faith and
love which are in Christ Jesus; ¹⁴ guard the truth that has been entrusted to
you by the Holy Spirit who dwells within us.

¹⁵ You are aware that all who are in Asia turned away from me, and
among them Phygelus and Hermogenes. ¹⁶ May the Lord grant mercy to
the household of Onesiphorus, for he often refreshed me; he was not ashamed
of my chains, ¹⁷ but when he arrived in Rome he searched for me eagerly
and found me – ¹⁸ may the Lord grant him to find mercy from the Lord on
that Day – and you well know all the service he rendered me at Ephesus.

ᵃOr what I have entrusted to him

The reader who turns to this Epistle after reading either I Timothy or Titus will notice few striking new themes. He will however sense a more strongly personal quality. There are more personal names, more references to people in Paul's and Timothy's circles, more allusions to details, even trivial details, of their circumstances. There are also more close reminiscences of those passages in Paul's undoubted letters which reflect his own calling and role. Yet beneath all this, which at first speaks so loudly in the cause of authenticity, the assumptions and the concerns to which the writer bears witness are those with which the reader of the other two letters is only too familiar. Only the expression is without a doubt more vivid, sometimes movingly so, at least in patches. In other words, the writer is going to greater pains here to imitate his model and to identify himself with him (there is room for much discussion which is the better description of his purpose), but he remains himself. The significance of these features of II Timothy is discussed on p. 32–5. All of them are prominent in the first chapter.

They are encapsulated in the reference to Timothy's mother and grandmother in v. 5. First, we have the reference to *sincere faith*. The words occur in I Timothy, in much the same position (1^5). But there the use is general – such faith is a requirement of Christian life. Here it is a quality in Timothy himself. More than that, he has inherited it from his mother and grandmother, both of them named. It is worth noting that it *dwelt first* in them: it is something he has taken over, not simply something he shares. We are presented not with a family of Christians, regarded as, in respect of their faith, contemporaries; but with three Christian generations, in effect almost a Christian clan. Here the widows (or their like), faceless in I Tim. 5, acquire individuality. Here the households delineated in I Tim. 3 and 5 receive shape, not to mention the devout women of I Tim. 2^{9ff}.. And implicit in their brief appearance is a feeling, not only of what already deserves to be called Christian family life, with all the stability inherent in that expression, but also of the possession of Christian roots. Except in his assumption of the mantle of Paul, our writer does not go out of his way to stress continuity with Christian origins. (We may contrast the writer of I John, in some of his references to the 'beginning', e.g. 2^7; 3^{11}.) He is nevertheless aware of his responsibility to maintain what has been entrusted to him: I Tim. 6^{20}; II Tim. 1^{14}.

And he is aware of belonging to a community which can already look to a past. Perhaps it is this awareness above all – membership of a substantial body, with a heritage to hold – which lies at the heart of our three letters.

Such a reading of course presupposes non-Pauline authorship. Yet a verse like 1^5, with its personal names (who would invent them?), is surely among the strongest arguments against it. In fact, for this purpose, the witness condemns himself as he enters the box. For what could be more unlike the circumstances of Paul and more like those of fifty or sixty years after his death than this casual reference to three generations in the faith, without so much as a hint of the conversion from either paganism or Judaism of any of the persons mentioned?

1

For the general form, which is closer to that in the opening greeting of I Timothy than of Titus, see p. 45. The expression *apostle of Christ Jesus by the will of God* reproduces exactly Paul's form in I Cor. 1^1; II Cor. 1^1; and Col. 1^1 (cf. also Eph. 1^1). It is a first symptom of the intensified 'paulineness' of this letter. I Tim. 1^1 has *command* instead of *will*.

promise of life: cf. I Tim. 4^8, where the Greek for the phrase is identical. There, a more literal rendering than RSV would be: 'having a promise of life which is both present and to come'; and the context shows that the reference is to simple existence, of course bestowed by God and Christian in character, but still temporally regarded. Here, the qualifying phrase, *which is in Christ Jesus*, appears both to 'paulinize' (cf. Rom. 8^2) and to spiritualize the word *life*. Surely it is now much more qualitative. But that qualitative sense (even more characteristic of the Johannine writings than of Paul) is not typical of our writer: four out of the eight uses of the word carry the adjective 'eternal', and in all these cases except I Tim. 6^{12} the reference is to future existence. The same is true of I Tim. 6^{19} and perhaps II Tim. 1^{10}. But does not *in Christ Jesus* firmly indicate a more spiritual or mystical sense? By comparison with genuine Paul, this expression is relatively rare in these writings, apart from II Timothy (once more the stronger Pauline colouring). It appears in I Tim. 1^{14}; 3^{13}; II Tim. 1^{9,13}; 2^{1,10}; 3^{12,15}. (The simple 'in Christ' does not occur at all.) But in some cases, it is used in connection with Christian qualities, like faith and love (e.g. I Tim. 1^{14} and II Tim. 1^{13}), and seems to say little more than that they are characteristic of Christian life. And as far as its use with *faith* is concerned (cf. in addition I Tim. 3¹³ and II Tim. 3¹⁵), the sense may well be that of 'belief in' or 'trust in', so that these are not true uses of the phrase. Except in a few cases, especially those with *grace* (II Tim. 1⁹ and 2¹), it is not easy to feel that our writer has quite grasped the deep Pauline sense of life in Christ as a new dimension of being. Rather, he sees life (present or future) as now capable of being Christian life, marked by new features as it continues within the old temporal framework. Not for the first time we suspect that a phrase which looks impressively Pauline conceals a quite un-Pauline flavour. And it is the use of the same phrase in other contexts, where the sense is plainer, which allows us to remove the (no doubt unwitting) disguise.

Apart from the meaning of the words, the construction of the verse as a whole is not entirely clear. Probably the sense is that the purpose of Paul's apostleship, willed by God, is to convey his promise of the new Christian life and to make possible its reception.

2

beloved: replaces *true* in I Tim. 1². Otherwise, apart from the omission of *in the faith*, the two verses are identical.

3

I thank God: here – and here alone in this group of writings – we have the customary thanksgiving in its customary place: see p. 50. It follows in these respects not only the secular but – more significantly – the general Pauline model. The content of the thanksgiving is intensely personal – more so than those in some of the genuine letters of Paul. It is almost a catena of allusions to personal, heartfelt passages in those letters. The aim is to impress upon the reader the strong authority of Paul, the pillar of traditional faith, whose own faith is built on deep foundations. The exhortation (v. 6f.) is intended to be powerful and unanswerable.

Both here and in I Tim. 1¹², the verb *thank* is not *eucharisteō*, which Paul uses in all his thanksgivings, but *charin echō*. It may be that by the time of writing, the former verb was acquiring sufficiently formal associations with liturgical, 'eucharistic' thanksgivings that it was better avoided where the ordinary sense was intended.

serve: Greek *latreuō*, the technical term for the service of God, particularly in worship but also more generally.

clear conscience: as in I Tim. 3⁹. For *conscience*, cf. p. 57. cf. Acts 23¹; 24¹⁶.

as did my fathers: lit. 'from (my) ancestors'. The word is the same as
that for *parents* in I Tim. 5⁴ (*progonoi*), but here the sense is clearly wider.
While the verse as a whole is reminiscent of Rom. 1⁹, this allusion looks
to passages like Rom. 11¹ and Phil. 3⁵. There, however, there is a turbu-
lent undercurrent in Paul's appeal to his Jewish ancestry. Here there is
only a sense of untroubled continuity. The tension involved in Paul's
movement from Judaism to Christ has been eliminated. For pseudo-
Paul, that issue is dead, at least as far as it concerned the life of Paul.

4

your tears: it may be far-fetched, but if 'Timothy' stands for the church
in Ephesus, and if the reference is to a specific occasion, then we may
see here evidence that the writer knew Acts 20³⁷, where the elders of
the Ephesian congregation weep at Paul's departure. Ephesus is seen as
Timothy's place (I Tim. 1³). However, the longing *to see you* reproduces Rom. 1¹¹, and the hoped for joy in the visit looks to Rom. 15³².
The conjunction of *tears* and *joy* is reminiscent of Paul in passages like
II Cor. 7⁸ᶠᶠ· and Phil. 2¹⁷; but the paradox is less sharp here.

night and day: the Greek allows this phrase to be taken with the *prayers*
of v. 3 rather than the longing.

5

sincere faith: cf. I Tim. 1⁵. The qualities referred to in a general way in
the First Letter are here, characteristically, attached to specific persons:
'Paul' has the *clear conscience*' (v. 3), 'Timothy' the *sincere faith*. The
second reference to his faith, at the end of the verse, seems redundant
in view of the first. But to applaud a quality in members of the flock,
then, not being quite sure, to urge its display is a device not uncommon
among pastors. It may be the effect intended here.

grandmother: Paul's ancestors (v. 3) are balanced by Timothy's. Both are
seen as men with roots, and there is no attempt to distinguish Jewish
from Christian background. The important thing is that the orthodox
stream is free from mere novelty. But as far as 'Timothy' (and therefore
the congregation) is concerned, there is also a concern with the place
of the Christian household in assuring the transmission of true faith.

mother: cf. Acts 16¹, where no name appears.

6

laying on of my hands: to what is this intended to refer? In the Acts pre-
sentation (16¹ᶠ·), Timothy is already a Christian when Paul first meets

him. This is not then a reference to his reception into the Church, unless our writer works without the Acts story. Nor does it seem to refer to his commissioning as head of the congregation, for that takes place when the elders lay hands on him: cf. I Tim. 4^{14}, which like our present verse refers to *the gift*. We have to face the question whether in these passages we are reading an account of actual institutions in the Church of the writer's time, if not before, or whether we are seeing evidence of his preoccupation with the handing on of true authority and authentic tradition. If we adopt the latter suggestion, then we are freed from the necessity of making an intelligible institutional pattern of the handlayings referred to. But if we see not only 'Timothy' and the elders but also 'Paul' as representing elements within the Church structure of the writer's day, then we need not find it inconceivable that there was an element of authorization from outside, by a figure responsible, no doubt, for a group of congregations, as well as from within. A picture of such groupings of congregations can be seen in the Johannine Epistles, probably in the Epistles of Ignatius, in the responsibility evinced in I Clement by the Roman church for the church in Corinth, and possibly in the picture in Acts of Paul's supervision of a number of congregations. It is hard to say whether our writer's primary interest is in doctrinal orthodoxy or in the ecclesiastical machinery which protects it, and whether his idiom is purely literary or also descriptive. cf. p. 89.

7

spirit of: the expression goes back to Isaiah 11^2; while none of the words of that passage appears here, 'strength' there matches *power*. There is closer – and odder – similarity with Rom. 8^{15}; 'the spirit of slavery (to fall back) into fear'. The idea of fear (different word) is in both passages; but the Greek for 'slavery' (*douleia*) is very close to our *timidity* (*deilia*) – as if our writer was working from a hazy recollection of the Romans passage. In view of both the Isaiah background ('the Spirit of the Lord') and the writer's other uses of *pneuma* (e.g. I Tim. 3^{16}; 4^1; Tit. 3^5), it is likely that the meaning of *spirit* is more concrete than appears at first glance: God's spirit issuing in the qualities mentioned, which are the specific content of *the gift* in v. 6.

self-control: Greek *sōphronismos*. The group of words to which this belongs is virtually confined to our writer in the New Testament (ten occurrences), and is thoroughly characteristic of his attitudes (cf. p. 70). However, Rom. 12^3 uses a cognate verb in a comparable sense.

8

ashamed: cf. vv. 12, 16. There is probably a reference to Rom. 1^{16} – the opening sections of Romans are constantly alluded to in this passage. It is typical that the sense is here made more concrete: where Paul is 'not ashamed of the Gospel', our writer thinks of the specific act of testifying, probably in court or on some other occasion of controversy. Language about 'shame' and 'being ashamed' is common in the New Testament in relation both to apostasy here and now and to acceptance by God on the Last Day; cf. e.g. Mark 8^{38}; I John 2^{28}. Here it is linked with the common Pauline theme of suffering as an essential and pervasive element in the apostle's vocation. In passages like II Cor. 4$^{7-12}$ and 12$^{8-10}$, it is worked out powerfully and profoundly: precisely in his suffering, the apostle is the vehicle of Christ's power. Here that deep and almost paradoxical sense is lacking. Rather, a *share of suffering* is just one aspect of a Christian leader's lot. It is presented here partly for that reason but perhaps more because it would be hard to give an intimate and personal communication from 'Paul' without this element, which is so prominent in the more personal parts of his own letters.

testifying: lit. 'the testimony', cf. I Tim. 2^6. It is hard to say how far this is part of the Pauline 'staging' of the letter, together with the references to his imprisonment (cf. 4$^{6ff.}$), or whether it refers to specific persecution in store for the recipients, such as Paul had once experienced. Apart from these more personal Pauline passages, the impression is given that the churches in mind in these letters live quiet lives, settled in an accepting society (cf. I Tim. 3^7). There is hardly an air of crisis. In that case, these references are part of a scenario of a now past heroic period, for whose recurrence the Christian must of course be prepared. For 'testimony' (*marturion*), beginning, with its associations of suffering, to shade into the idea of martyrdom, cf. pp. 69, 101.

his prisoner: see p. 33. cf. Phil. 1^7; Philem. 1, 9; Col. 4^{18}; Eph. 3^1. It is better to treat this as part of the Pauline realism typical of this writing than to attempt to find a specific place for it in the biography of Paul. It contributes to the solemnity of the message which comes from the heroic leader's pen.

take your share of suffering: a single Greek word, *sunkakopatheō*, otherwise only in 2^3. Compounds with the preposition *sun* (with) are a favourite with Paul, but this one does not occur in his work.

power of God: the collocation of this phrase with *be ashamed* and *gospel* is present also in Rom. 1[16].

9

saved: cf. p. 60. This unambiguous use of this word for what God has already done is rare in Paul (Rom. 8[24]). It occurs in Tit. 3[5]; cf. also Eph. 2[5,8] and perhaps I Tim. 1[15]. Elsewhere in the Pastoral Epistles, it refers more probably to the future; the same is true of *salvation*, II Tim. 2[10] and 3[15].

called ... calling: for verb and noun together, cf. Eph. 4[1,4]. For the theme, cf. Rom. 8[28-30]; I Cor. 1[9]. Note the appearance of the two verbs, *save* and *call*, in the same passage in Rom. 8; also *purpose*.

in virtue of our works: lit. 'according to our works'; cf. for the phrase Rom. 2[6]; and for the thought Rom. 3[20,28]; 4[6]. This central Pauline theme appears in the Pastorals only here and in Tit. 3[5].

gave ... ago: There is a close similarity to Rom. 16[25f.], which continues in the following verse. The idea that God gave his grace to his chosen ones *in Christ Jesus ages ago* cannot be said to be characteristic of this writer. It may be no more than an expansion of the idea of God's purpose, as far as our writer is concerned, but expressed in a form taken over from Rom. 16. It is surely unlikely that he is implying a developed doctrine of Christ's pre-existence. Rather, God foresaw the salvation now given through Christ. The Greek *ages ago* uses the same two words as *for long ages* in Rom. 16[25].

Clearly this verse and v. 10 are designed to present a strong and formal statement of Pauline doctrine, comparable, in these writings, to Tit. 3[4-7]. Both passages have something of the air of a manifesto. Leaning heavily on Paul, they rise above the normal run of the writer's teaching. In particular, his fundamentally moralistic cast of mind is not greatly concerned with the issue of faith or works which was so central to Paul. Here, while some of the right language appears, the point is made in a way that is just non-Pauline: *works* are contrasted not with faith, but with two somewhat disparate words – *purpose* and *grace*, neither of which would make the usual Pauline contrast. The preposition *kata* is used with all three nouns loosely, lit. 'according to'. The contrast here is between 'our' *works* and 'his', God's, *purpose and grace*. The actual language of v. 10 is more characteristic of this writer.

10

appearing: Greek *epiphaneia.* cf. I Tim. 6^{14}; II Tim. 4^{1,8}; Tit. 2^{13}. Here only the word refers to Christ's first coming.

Saviour: cf. p. 47. Again, a word hitherto usually applied to Christ at his expected return (cf. the use of 'save', p. 60), as for example in Paul's only use of it, in Phil. 3^{20}; but now, with no sense of strain, it is applied to Christ's first coming. Alongside this development, we find in these writings no sense of impending crisis in relation to the future return of Christ, his second 'epiphany'. It is assured, but there is no worry about the timing of it.

abolished death: cf. I Cor. 15^{26}.

life and immortality: immortality is an attribute of God in I Tim. 6^{16} – and of him alone. But the word there is *athanasia.* Here it is *aphtharsia,* more strictly 'incorruption', 'imperishability'; all three ideas were most intimately linked. What is of greater interest is that immortality is seen as a Christian gift rather then resurrection. In the absence of any statement to the contrary, we may suppose that our writer saw Christians as having this gift from the moment of death (*life* leading to *immortality*). No wonder then that the delay in the coming of Christ at the End caused no anxiety. We may contrast Paul, for whom this gift only comes with the event of resurrection, at the End: cf. I Cor. 15^{42}. In this, Paul is closer to traditional Judaism; but our writer's pattern is not impossible in Judaism by this period, cf. Wis. 2^{23}; 3^4; IV Maccabees 14^5; 17^{12}.* For *life* in these writings, see pp. 60, 107.

11

I was appointed etc.: cf. I Tim. 2^7.

12

suffer: cf. above, on v. 8.

not ashamed: cf. above, on v. 8.

what has been entrusted to me: lit. 'my deposit', cf. I Tim. 6^{20} – which surely indicates that the sense is as in the text and not as in the margin. Christ himself will protect the authentic teaching from perversion.

*Charles, II, p. 653.

13

pattern: Greek *hupotupōsis*, rendered *example* in I Tim. 1[16].

sound words: cf. I Tim, 6[3]; also I Tim. 1[10]. One of our writer's chief themes.

faith and love: cf. I Tim. 1[14].
It is notable how, once our writer leaves the personal Pauline scenario, he reverts to well-trodden paths.

14
cf. I Tim. 6[20].

15–18
What is the point of this passage? If the letter were Pauline, it would read like mere personal gossip, of a kind rare in the Pauline letters. Only in Philemon and Col. 4 is there much material with which it can be compared; other references to persons are either greetings or concerned with travel plans. If it is not authentic Paul, then perhaps this is simply another patch of strong colour, adding verisimilitude to the epistolary form. But the personal language of the earliest part of the chapter was a more vivid way of presenting some of the writer's important teaching, his sense of authentic tradition and leadership in the Church, given in more impersonal form in I Timothy. So now the personal details express another of his major concerns: the fight against heresy.

15
all: an exaggeration designed to heighten the heroic picture of Paul; cf. 4[10ff.].

turned away: in 4[4] and Tit. 1[14], the same verb, *apostrephō*, is used of turning away into false doctrine, and probably it has that strong sense here. We have no other references to Phygelus or Hermogenes.

16
not ashamed: once more, as in v. 15, it is likely that other than social relationships are in mind. Note the link between 'not being ashamed' and bearing witness in v. 8. *The household of Onesiphorus* stands for the exemplary, orthodox Christians. They appear again in 4[19]. We are told nothing of the fate of Onesiphorus himself, but, like Epaphroditus in

Phil. 2^{25} (was he the model?) he is presented as one whose devotion to Paul went as far as following him to Rome (presumably the period covered at the end of Acts is in mind). Our writer seeks to foster such devotion to the master.

18

the Lord: the awkward repetition of the word may derive from the inefficient combining of pious formulas.

2$^{1-13}$ THE GLORIOUS DUTY OF SUFFERING

¹ You then, my son, be strong in the grace that is in Christ Jesus, ² and what you have heard from me before many witnesses entrust to faithful men who will be able to teach others also. ³ Take your share of suffering as a good soldier of Christ Jesus. ⁴ No soldier on service gets entangled in civilian pursuits, since his aim is to satisfy the one who enlisted him. ⁵ An athlete is not crowned unless he competes according to the rules. ⁶ It is the hardworking farmer who ought to have the first share of the crops. ⁷ Think over what I say, for the Lord will grant you understanding in everything.

⁸ Remember Jesus Christ, risen from the dead, descended from David, as preached in my gospel, ⁹ the gospel for which I am suffering and wearing fetters like a criminal. But the word of God is not fettered. ¹⁰ Therefore I endure everything for the sake of the elect, that they also may obtain the salvation which in Christ Jesus goes with eternal glory. ¹¹ The saying is sure:

> *If we have died with him, we shall also live with him;*
> *¹² if we endure, we shall also reign with him;*
> *if we deny him, he also will deny us;*
> *¹³ if we are faithless, he remains faithful –*
> *for he cannot deny himself.*

The first two verses make a transition from the last part of chapter one, as the connecting word *then* (in fact stronger – 'therefore', *oun*) shows. The view we have taken of that passage is thus confirmed: 'Timothy' is to be like Onesiphorus and that means handing on the true teaching (v. 2). The contrast between Onesiphorus on the one hand and Phygelus and Hermogenes on the other is therefore not concerned with personal support but rather with orthodoxy and heresy.

The following of the true pattern of life also means embracing suffering. Now Paul rather than Onesiphorus is the model, and the rest of the passage takes up $1^{8,16}$, where the theme has already been announced. It does not arise at all in the portraits of Christian behaviour given in the more general I Timothy and Titus. The question arises how far there is a certain artificiality about this piece of exhortation. The picture in the other writings is one of peaceful, continuing Church life. Is this talk of heroic suffering, embellished with military imagery, then rather like the popularity of uniformed organizations in the latter days of the long Victorian peace in England? Is it, like 'Onward, Christian soldiers', a hankering after a model of Christian life whose appeal arose precisely because it had so little contact with reality? This would confirm the view that II Timothy, with its more personal picture of both apostle and followers, deliberately looks to the heroic model as the basis for exhortation. Look back to those splendid times, it says, and stir yourselves for vigilant Christian life in these more humdrum days.

'Timothy' is to see suffering as part of his calling just as 'Paul' did. As we have seen (p. 111), this idea is central to Paul's concept of apostleship. In Paul himself, there is a sense in which identification with Christ in suffering is characteristic particularly of the apostle, and it is chiefly in that context that Paul explores this rich vein of thought. However, it does extend to all Christians, as Rom. 8^{17} shows. It is unclear how far our writer has believers in general in mind in v. 3ff. or whether he is thinking particularly of Christian leaders.

There is a difference of nuance from Paul's treatment of the theme. For Paul, the Christian's suffering is the fruit of his mystical identity with Christ. And there is a kind of balance, whereby the apostle's afflictions are the necessary means for both the revelation of Christ's power (II Cor. 4^{11}) and the strengthening of the believers (II Cor. 4^{12}; $13^{ff.}$). The negative is the key to the positive. Here the pattern is much simpler. There is no mention of Christ's sufferings; instead the model of suffering is Paul (1^8), while Christ is a purely 'positive' figure, who 'appears', both in the past to abolish death (1^{10}) and in the future in glory (Tit. 2^{13}), and is the source of the life and faith of his followers. Suffering then takes its place as part of the essential Christian discipline, an element in taking one's faith seriously. The concept is less profound than that of Paul, less paradoxical and more clear-cut. We have embarked on the long history of straightforward Christian discipline.

🜲

1 f.

You, then: we have taken this (see above) to connect with the immediately preceding passage: 'Timothy' is to *be strong in grace* as, by his practical conduct, Onesiphorus so abundantly showed himself to be. But v. 2 looks back beyond the practical illustration which that passage provides to the sentiments of $1^{13f.}$.

many witnesses: cf. I Tim. 6^{12}. The solemn congregational setting appeals to our writer and is familiar to him, whether, as in the I Timothy passage, for baptism or, as here, for ordination.

entrust: 'Timothy's' ordination – seen as his commissioning to hold and teach the true faith – is set within a continuing process of tradition. I Clem. 42, 44 (*ECW*, p. 45f.) presents a comparable picture but has a more formal sense of transmission and a more general sense of the apostolic fount of the teaching. But the idea is as early as Paul himself: cf. I Cor. 15^3.

3–7

soldier: cf. I Tim. 1^{18}, p. 62. Paul uses this image for the Christian in Phil. 2^{25} and Philem.², and, momentarily, for another purpose in I Cor. 9^7. But it is not exploited with the vividness of, for example, the Qumran *War Rule*★ or even of Eph. $6^{10ff.}$.

athlete: a second image. cf. perhaps I Tim. 6^{12}, p. 100. Also I Cor. 9^{24-7}. In Paul the stress is on strenuous effort to achieve; here on competing *according to the rules*. This means in effect accepting the conditions of the enterprise – in the case of 'Timothy', the Christian task and discipline. The shift is striking and wholly characteristic. For our writer, to be a Christian is to accept a pattern and stick to it.

farmer: I Cor. 9 (in vv. 7, 9–12) has the agricultural as well as the athletic and military images, but our writer uses them more briefly and side

★Vermes, p. 122ff.

by side. The similarity of wording between v. 6 and I Cor. 9[10] is less close in the Greek than RSV implies. The thought has moved from v. 4f. and is nearer to (though more general than) the Pauline parallel: virtue should be rewarded. cf. Deut. 20[6]. The idea of discipline, in its two aspects of conformity to a system and intensity of effort, unites the three images. All three are commonplace, though their presence here is probably by way of Paul.

8

risen: as in 1[9f.], we have now a brief set of doctrinal statements, all echoing Paul. The first is close to I Cor. 15[20]; cf. also Rom. 1[4]. What we have here is no more than a slogan – no doctrinal use is made of the fact of Christ's resurrection.

descended from David: cf. Rom. 1[3], Paul's only reference to this matter. Ignatius also took it up: Trallians 9 (*ECW*, p. 97) and Smyrneans 1 (*ECW*, p. 119).

as preached in my gospel: lit. 'according to my gospel', reproducing exactly Rom. 2[16] and 16[25], a passage already used in 1[9f.]. At first sight, the two affirmations concerning Christ here selected as typifying the writer's gospel seem a little arbitrary, but if we take them as representing Christ's heavenly and earthly aspects then they correspond to the two sets of statements which make up the formula in I Tim. 3[16], to which, whether it was his own work or not, our writer clearly attached great importance.

9

gospel for which I am suffering: cf. Phil. 1[12-14]. He takes up Paul's theme that not even imprisonment can stifle the gospel (*the word of God*).

10

the elect: God's people, chosen for salvation. The idea stretches back to the theology of Israel. Paul has the term in Rom. 8[33]; 16[13]; Col. 3[12].

also: i.e. as well as Paul. The idea of the apostle suffering for the Christians is in Col. 1[24]. All the other references to *glory* in these writings (e.g. I Tim. 1[11] and Tit. 2[13]) see it as a property of God. For the idea of believers sharing in glory, i.e. the splendour of heaven, cf. Rom. 8[21,30]; II Cor. 3[18]; and John 17[22].

11-13

saying is sure: cf. p. 59f. This four-line piece (taking v. 13b to be a comment added by the writer) has the look of a quoted formula, perhaps a hymn. However, it cannot be claimed that it is seriously out of line with the cast of thought displayed in the rest of these writings. The idea of denying God recurs in Tit. 1^{16}, though the language of 'not being ashamed' is commoner. The thought of reigning with Christ is a little dramatic for this writer – though it may be implicit in the sharing of glory in v. 10. On the other hand, faithfulness is a prime virtue in these works. Therefore it is a moot point whether these lines come from the writer himself or from his stock of revered formulas. The same problem arises with his other 'faithful sayings'. That we are dealing with a known formula may be indicated by the close similarity with Polycarp, Philippians 5 (*ECW*, p. 146) – though our judgement will be affected by the view taken of the relationship between the two writers, see p. 42. It is possible that the piece took its origin from Rom. 6^8, with which the first line is virtually identical; taking that line as the *point de départ*, the rest developed.

The movement of the thought of the piece supports the view that it is an integral part of the writing rather than a quotation inserted; for it can be seen to provide a bridge from what precedes to what follows. The first two lines express the theme of suffering and its fruits; the rest expresses the related theme of loyalty, which then leads into the attack on heresy, against which such loyalty is the great weapon, recognized by God (cf. v. 19).

if we deny: cf. Matt. 10^{33}. The idea is common enough for it to be impossible to be sure whether a traditional saying of Jesus is being quoted. On the face of it, v. 12b and v. 13a contradict each other, and v. 13b seeks to elucidate the matter, by providing a paradox. But it is partly a matter of 'when': if we deny him, he will deny us – at the Last Day (cf. 1^{18}; 2^{10}); on the other hand, our faithlessness does not deter God from faithfulness to his covenant and his purpose, chiefly now (cf. Rom. 3$^{3f.}$, which may be in mind). It is also a matter of 'who': v. 12b has in mind the individual believer and his fate, v. 13a the purpose of God for his people in general.

¹⁴ *Remind them of this, and charge them before the Lord*[b] *to avoid disputing about words, which does no good, but only ruins the hearers.* ¹⁵ *Do your best to present yourself to God as one approved, a workman who has no need to be ashamed, rightly handling the word of truth.* ¹⁶ *Avoid such godless chatter, for it will lead people into more and more ungodliness,* ¹⁷ *and their talk will eat its way like gangrene. Among them are Hymenaeus and Philetus,* ¹⁸ *who have swerved from the truth by holding that the resurrection is past already. They are upsetting the faith of some.* ¹⁹ *But God's firm foundation stands, bearing this seal: 'The Lord knows who are his', and, 'Let every one who names the name of the Lord depart from iniquity'.*

²⁰ *In a great house there are not only vessels of gold and silver but also of wood and earthenware, and some for noble use, some for ignoble.* ²¹ *If anyone purifies himself from what is ignoble, then he will be a vessel for noble use, consecrated and useful to the master of the house, ready for any good work.* ²² *So shun youthful passion and aim at righteousness, faith, love, and peace, along with those who call upon the Lord from a pure heart.* ²³ *Have nothing to do with stupid, senseless controversies; you know that they breed quarrels.* ²⁴ *And the Lord's servant must not be quarrelsome but kindly to every one, an apt teacher, forbearing,* ²⁵ *correcting his opponents with gentleness. God may perhaps grant that they will repent and come to know the truth,* ²⁶ *and they may escape from the snare of the devil, after being captured by him to do his will*[c].

[b]Other ancient authorities read *God*. [c]Or *by him, to do his* (that is God's) *will*.

We turn to the other side of the coin. The Christian leader must stick firm to his commission, maintaining the truth, if necessary suffering for it. That means attacking false doctrine and cultivating the moral qualities which the proper conduct of the struggle demands (cf. vv. 21–6). There is still hope that the heretics will repent: the lines are not yet fixed.

This purpose unifies the passage which at first sight seems to lapse into a somewhat random collection of moral recommendations.

𝓏

14

them: not expressed in the Greek with either verb. The natural object is *the elect* of v. 10, i.e. the faithful believers.

disputing about words: cf. I Tim. 6⁴·²⁰. In the former of those passages there is a contrast with the *sound words* of the true faith, which is implicit here. This group of words (Greek *logomacheō*, etc.) occurs only in these writings in the New Testament. Perhaps only this writer felt so strongly antipathetic to anything like speculative theology and was so apt to class discussion as 'mere talk'. He is clear that there is a fixed pattern of teaching which can only suffer from attempts to tamper with it. *God* is probably the better reading.

15

a workman ... rightly handling: another image making the same point as those in v. 4ff. What is required is the workaday virtue of sticking to one's last – fulfilling the requirements. Such a one has no need to feel shame before God (cf. v. 15a) or indeed before men (cf. 1⁸). The verb translated *rightly handling* (*orthotomein*) is found elsewhere only in the LXX of Prov. 5⁶ and 11⁵, with the object 'paths', and the sense 'cut straight paths'. A & G suggest for our passage: 'guide the word of truth along a straight path', i.e. avoiding diversion into wordy debate.

the word of truth: cf. Eph. 1¹³.

16

chatter: cf. I Tim. 6²⁰.

ungodliness: Greek *asebeia*, cf. p. 59.

17

eat its way: but there is determination to resist, cf. 3⁹. Or perhaps the idea is that in affected individuals it goes from bad to worse, cf. 3¹³.

Hymenaeus: cf. I Tim. 1²⁰, where a man of this name has a different partner. These are men formerly faithful, now in error, still possessing influence, cf. v. 18b. If the names are fictitious, or taken over from tradition, then no doubt these statements merely describe situations current in the Church at the time of writing.

18

resurrection is past: an important error is identified. (It appears only here and others are mentioned elsewhere, cf. I Tim. 4³.) Both Pauline and Johannine Christians might be accused of it: Rom. 6³⁻¹¹; Col. 3¹; John 5²⁴; I John 3¹⁴. Intense Christian life produced this conviction that the 'risen' state was anticipated here and now. Some of Paul's Christians already took it too far: he may be attacking teaching of this over-spiritual kind in I Cor. 15.* This aspect of Gnostic contempt for the realities of material bodily existence, and sense of salvation as total conquest of them, appears more clearly in the (probably) second century work, *The Epistle to Rheginos*,† and it is indeed a familiar feature of Gnostic teaching. Our writer pushes the Pauline tradition firmly away from such doctrine.

19

foundation: cf. I Tim. 3¹⁵. The image is used here in a general sense, but it was already familiar in Christian use. In particular, Paul used it of Christ (I Cor. 3¹¹) and in Ephesians (2²⁰) it is applied to the apostles and prophets. There is no reason to think that either is in mind here. Behind this common New Testament imagery may well lie Isaiah 28¹⁶, which is actually quoted a number of times, in particular in Rom. 9³³ (cf. the use of Rom. 9²¹ in v. 20ff.).

seal: part of the foundation-stone image. It is the inscription on the stone, stating its purpose. There follow two appropriate scriptural statements: the first is from the LXX of Num. 16⁵; the second appears to combine Num. 16²⁶ and perhaps Isaiah 26¹³ and 52¹¹, but only loosely, in the manner of Jewish exegesis. The story of the apostates, Korah, Dathan and Abiram, with which Num. 16 is concerned, is suitably drawn upon here.‡

20f.

vessels: cf. Rom. 9²¹, which gave our writer his starting-point for the use of this image (cf. also Wis. 15⁷). But here there is no question of God's election which is the theme of Rom. 9: it is a matter of effort and good conduct. One may purify oneself *from what is ignoble.* The reference to vessels for noble and ignoble use echoes I Cor. 12²²ᶠ·, where

---

* See C. K. Barrett, *The First Epistle to the Corinthians*, A. & C. Black, 1968, p. 347ff.

† M. L. Peel (ed.), SCM, 1969, p. 140ff.

‡ See A. T. Hanson, op. cit., ch. 3.

the vocabulary is the same (the *timē*, 'honour', group of words). But the point of that passage, that all have their place, is ignored. The message here is not doctrinal but hortatory. And the contrast is not that of Paul in Rom. 9, between Christians and rejected Jews, but, typically, between orthodox and apostates.

youthful passions: cf. I Tim. 4¹². Addressed to 'Timothy', but presumably occasioned by the needs of young men in positions of leadership in the Church by the time of writing.

righteousness etc.: cf. I Tim. 6¹¹.

23
controversies: the writer has told us little about their content (but cf. v. 18). It is the fact of them and their disturbing effect which trouble him. His object is peaceful and stable Church life.

quarrels: Greek *machai*; cf. the compound *logomacheō* in v. 14.

24
servant: in particular, the congregation's leader.

apt teacher: cf. I Tim. 3².

25
repent: i.e. of holding false doctrine, which overlaps for this writer with contentiousness.

26
snare of the devil: cf. I Tim. 3⁷.

captured: Greek *zōgreō*; only here and in Lk. 5¹⁰.

3¹⁻¹⁷   HERESY AND SIN

¹ *But understand this, that in the last days there will come times of stress.* ² *For men will be lovers of self, lovers of money, proud, arrogant, abusive, disobedient to their parents, ungrateful, unholy,* ³ *inhuman, implacable, slanderers, profligates, fierce, haters of good,* ⁴ *treacherous, reckless, swollen with conceit, lovers of pleasure rather than lovers of God,* ⁵ *holding the form of religion but denying the power of it. Avoid such people.* ⁶ *For among*

them are those who make their way into households and capture weak women, burdened with sins and swayed by various impulses, 7 who will listen to anybody and can never arrive at a knowledge of the truth. 8 As Jannes and Jambres opposed Moses, so these men also oppose the truth, men of corrupt mind and counterfeit faith; 9 but they will not get very far, for their folly will be plain to all, as was that of those two men.

10 Now you have observed my teaching, my conduct, my aim in life, my faith, my patience, my love, my steadfastness, 11 my persecutions, my sufferings, what befell me at Antioch, at Iconium, and at Lystra, what persecutions I endured; yet from them all the Lord rescued me. 12 Indeed all those who desire to live a godly life in Christ Jesus will be persecuted, 13 while evil men and imposters will go on from bad to worse, deceivers and deceived. 14 But as for you, continue in what you have learned and have firmly believed, knowing from whom you learned it 15 and how from childhood you have been acquainted with the sacred writings which are able to instruct you for salvation through faith in Christ Jesus. 16 All scripture is inspired by God and[d] *profitable for teaching, for reproof, for correction, and for training in righteousness, 17 that the man of God may be complete, equipped for every good work.*

[d]*Or Every scripture inspired by God is also*

Heresy and sin go hand in hand, and that is to be expected when the End is not very far away. The First Epistle of John makes exactly the same point (especially in 2[18ff.]), though for that writer heresy itself and the schism that results are themselves the heart of sin, because they mean breaking the bond of brotherly love. Our writer ranges more widely in his censures. In fact, the evils listed in vv. 2–5 look like a purely general compilation rather than the result of observation of particular persons. Nevertheless, even if that list draws upon conventional material, it is plain that the heretics of the time are firmly in mind, partly at least (*among them*, v. 6). By v. 7 we are back on the familiar track of the condemnation of false teaching.

In these first verses, the wider social scene also seems to be in view: the nearness of the End is of cosmic significance and the general prevalence of sinfulness is a recognized sign that it will not be long delayed. In this sense, our writer's horizon is wider than that of I John, where the wickedness of schism in his congregation is the only evidence he notices.

As in 1⁸ᶠᶠ·, the contrasting exhortation takes the form of an appeal to Paul's example. He is the model both in his virtues and in his sufferings willingly endured. At the end of the passage, the scriptures of the Old Testament are introduced for the first time as an important element in the formation of the pattern of true doctrine.

1

the last days: cf. I Tim. 4¹. It was common doctrine that the time before the End would be characterized by unprecedented outbreaks of wickedness and disaster; cf. Mark 13¹⁴ᶠᶠ·; Rev. 18; and, from the Qumran Jews, The Commentary on Habakkuk, II,* where apostasy particularly is envisaged, as in our writer and in I John.

2–4

In Greek, some of the words are nicely paired by sound, e.g. the first two, *philautoi, philarguroi*; and eight in a run of nine begin with *a*. There is a certain random quality about this list which is nevertheless conventional, at least in form (for similar lists, cf. Rom. 1²⁹ᶠ· and Col. 3⁵). But some of the sins condemned echo other parts of the Pastoral Epistles: e.g. *lovers of money,* cf. I Tim. 3³; *disobedient to their parents,* cf. I Tim. 5⁴; *ungrateful,* I Tim. 4⁴; *haters of good,* Tit. 1⁸. These, and some (but not all) of the other vices, are either qualities whose opposites are particularly recommended for Christian leaders or noted features of the behaviour of the heretics.

5

The heretics come more directly before us in this verse. They are accused of having a deceptive outward semblance of true faith. Not everyone is able to see that their false doctrine denies the Lord who alone gives strength to his people (cf. 2¹²). For a warning against the same danger, cf. Matt. 7¹⁵,²¹.

6.

into households etc: perhaps we can see here something of the reason for the careful and protective regulations laid down for widows in I Tim. 5: cf. also I Tim. 2¹¹. For an example of this activity, see the Valentinian Gnostic work, Ptolemaeus' *Letter to Flora,*† in which a Gnostic teacher

*Vermes, p. 233.
†R. M. Grant (ed.), *Gnosticism*, Collins, 1961, pp. 184–90.

is opening up the process of instructing a woman keenly interested in religion.

8

Jannes and Jambres: in 2¹⁹ there was a reference to the exemplary story from the Jewish Law, concerning Korah and his associates. Now we have another reference to a story from the Pentateuch, that of Moses' struggles with the Egyptian magicians, cf. Ex. 7¹¹. Both stories were favourites with Jewish theologians of the time. This one served to point up the contrast between Judaism and the astrologers popular in this period. Christians also needed to differentiate between themselves and magical activity of various kinds, as the prominence of this motif in our sources indicates; cf. Matt. 2¹ff.; Acts 8⁹ff.; Ignatius, Ephesians 19 (*ECW*, p. 81).* Jewish tradition appears to have already given these names to the Egyptian wizards. 'Jannes and his brother' appear in the *Damascus Rule* as agents of Satan (Vermes, p. 102). Their trade helps to taint the Gnostic opponents with the air of exotic and speculative eccentricity for which our writer has so little time (cf. I Tim. 1⁴).

11

persecutions: another appeal to Paul the hero, cf. 1⁸; 2⁸ff.. We look to passages in Paul like II Cor. 6⁴⁻⁶; 11²³ff.. But whether our writer was looking to such references in the writings of Paul or to stories known to him in Acts or to both is the question raised by the reference to three towns in which Paul suffered. But perhaps that reference needs a different explanation.

Antioch, Iconium and Lystra: though we have found a number of points of contact with the outlook and even the language of Acts, this is the first passage which compels us to consider the possibility of literary dependence. The comparison is with Acts 13–14, the so-called first missionary journey of Paul, during which he visits these towns, among others. It is only concerning his stay in these places that formal stories are related. It is of course possible that both the writer of Acts and our writer happened both to know of Paul's troubles in these cities, and our writer happened to choose them as examples, perhaps because they were conveniently placed together in the same geographical area. It speaks against dependence on Acts that 'Timothy' is apparently thought to have been present on these occasions (*you have observed*, v. 10), and his appearance in Acts is not until ch. 16. So does the choice of these

*See also John M. Hull, *Hellenistic Magic and the Synoptic Tradition*, SCM, 1974.

three examples, when Acts contains so many that are more striking – unless it was simply that they come first in the story of Paul's travels. The possibility therefore arises that the dependence was the other way round; that the author of Acts took this reference as the skeleton for his account in chs. 13–14 and perhaps told stories only about these towns because they were the three specifically mentioned in his source. Pauline authorship would of course in a sense cut the knot, though the selection of just these examples would still be strange; a pseudonymous writer may look for no more than a little convincing local colour. If the view that Acts used II Timothy were to be accepted, it would have important implications for the relative dating of the two works and, presumably, for the date by which the Pastoral Epistles were accepted as Pauline.★

13

deceivers and deceived: cf. I Tim, 4¹; II Tim. 2²⁶. It is likely, from these comparisons, that supernatural agency is in mind. The combination of the two words is not uncommon in ancient literature.

15

from childhood: cf. 1⁵; p. 106. It reflects the writer's concept of stable tradition in the Christian family and cannot be drawn from Acts 16¹ff.

the sacred writings: Greek *hiera grammata:* Hellenistic Judaism's (especially Philo's) regular term for the Old Testament scriptures. Apart from a small number of excursions into Jewish-type exegesis, developing Old Testament texts in the manner of contemporary midrash (cf. I Tim. 2¹³·; 5¹⁸; II Tim. 2¹⁹),† our writer is not notable for his use of the Old Testament. He hardly ever quotes it directly, less than almost any early Christian writer. Yet here, rather abruptly, he commends it as a source of instruction *for salvation.* It might be said that he thus treats it in a way comparable to his view of the Christian faith; as a solid whole whose detailed content is disclosed only occasionally. It cannot be said that we get in these writings a very full picture of Christian belief as the writer saw it, any more than we are told much of what he considered to be so valuable in the Old Testament. But we are left in no doubt

★ See J. L. Keedy, unpublished doctoral thesis on *St Luke's Account of the Travels of St Paul,* Oxford, 1970, p. 41ff.
† See also A. T. Hanson, op. cit., ch. 4. A *bon mot* with regard to this verse notes that it is the mark of a mediocre mind to revere so highly that which is so little exploited.

that both the Christian teaching – and now the old scriptures – must be maintained at all costs.

Like other passages in these writings (e.g. I Tim. 1[8], *the law*), and indeed their stance as a whole, this verse shows no sense of the transition from Judaism or of any need to define a relationship with it – though *through faith in Christ Jesus* (in no way emphasized) may signify 'when understood in a Christian way'. Christianity seems to be regarded as already a self-contained, independent entity, which has absorbed its Jewish heritage without further need of discussion or controversy. The reference to *Jewish myths* in Tit. 1[14] does not invalidate this: what our writer sees as 'myths', whatever their source, Jewish or Christian, are rejected by him; and it is their foolish content rather than their Jewish origin which he finds objectionable.

16

all scripture: Greek *pasa graphē*; either 'all scripture' or 'every scripture' – i.e. each text. Both senses of *graphē* are found in other New Testament writers, including Paul. The former is preferable if the effects listed are to be taken seriously. No Christian of this period shows signs of appealing to any and every item of the Old Testament. On the contrary, they seem to have been highly selective. 'All scripture' thus accords better with contemporary Christian realities, and we have suggested above how our writer's mind may have moved in expressing itself so; it is more understandable than the alternative. True, he expounds a small handful of texts – and with ingenuity; but even with his attachment to matters of detail, he would scarcely (would he?) see them as providing items of instruction *for salvation*.

inspired: the Greek could yield (cf. the margin) 'Every inspired passage of scripture is also profitable . . .' But the implication that some parts of the Old Testament are not inspired cannot be intended in view of the case which the writer is advocating. The teaching is that the Old Testament as a whole is *inspired by God*. We may suppose that the heretics were selective in their use of Scripture – in effect (see above), that they made a different selection of texts from the orthodox, or perhaps that they lacked any concept of 'the Old Testament as a whole'. However, this is not necessarily being put forward as a strong feature of the opposition party's outlook; rather, the value of Scripture is stated positively, as part of the equipment of those who have a sense of fidelity to the true tradition. It is going beyond the evidence (though not impossible) to see the teaching of Marcion under fire here (cf. p. 102 on I Tim. 6[20]).*

The idea of the inspiration of Scripture is inherited from Judaism. It was held in a particularly strong form by Philo, by whom those who speak in the Old Testament are seen as possessed by God's spirit. Like our writer, with his *inspired* (*theopneustos*), he uses characteristically a word of the *pneuma* ('spirit') family (*katapneustheis*). II Peter, another early Christian writing with close affinities to Hellenistic Judaism, has the same strong doctrine of inspiration as our writer, cf. 1[20f.], and may even see in Balaam's ass the vehicle of divine inspiration, 2[15f.], as rabbis were to do. A. T. Hanson† points to the interesting relationship between our passage and Rom. 15[4-6]. He notes that Paul's idea of the authority of Scripture is strengthened and formalized in the direction of a doctrine of inspiration after the manner of Philo; and that some of the chief words in Paul's passage are taken up and transposed into our writer's typical key. Thus, Paul's *steadfastness* may have turned into the more Hellenistic *training*, Greek *paideia* (cf. our writer's easy use of military and athletic imagery, 2[4f.]); Paul's *encouragement* (his favourite *paraklēsis*) into the more moralistic *correction*. Both *reproof* and *correction* have in view the fight against the heretics. Another example of our writer's use of Romans.

17

man of God: i.e. probably, the Christian leader rather than the believer in general. Early sign of clericalism, and in line with the writer's tendency. cf. I Tim. 6[11].

good work: cf. I Tim. 2[10]. The object of absorption in the scriptures is both doctrinal and ethical. It is to produce the rounded Christian (leader).

4[1-22]   PAUL'S TESTAMENT

[1] *I charge you in the presence of God and of Christ Jesus who is to judge the living and the dead, and by his appearing and his kingdom:* [2] *preach the word, be urgent in season and out of season, convince, rebuke, and exhort,*

*For a more Christocentric approach to the question of scripture, see Ignatius, Philad., 8, *ECW*, p. 114.

†op. cit., pp. 52-4.

be unfailing in patience and in teaching. ³ *For the time is coming when people will not endure sound teaching, but having itching ears they will accumulate for themselves teachers to suit their own likings,* ⁴ *and will turn away from listening to the truth and wander into myths.* ⁵ *As for you, always be steady, endure suffering, do the work of an evangelist, fulfil your ministry.*

⁶ *For I am already on the point of being sacrificed; the time of my departure has come.* ⁷ *I have fought the good fight, I have finished the race, I have kept the faith.* ⁸ *Henceforth there is laid up for me the crown of righteousness, which the Lord, the righteous judge, will award to me on that Day, and not only to me but also to all who have loved his appearing.*

⁹ *Do your best to come to me soon.* ¹⁰ *For Demas, in love with this present world, has deserted me and gone to Thessalonica; Crescens has gone to Galatia*ᵉ, *Titus to Dalmatia.* ¹¹ *Luke alone is with me. Get Mark and bring him with you; for he is very useful in serving me.* ¹² *Tychicus I have sent to Ephesus.* ¹³ *When you come, bring the cloak that I left with Carpus at Troas, also the books, and above all the parchments.* ¹⁴ *Alexander the coppersmith did me great harm; the Lord will requite him for his deeds.* ¹⁵ *Beware of him yourself, for he strongly opposed our message.* ¹⁶ *At my first defence no one took my part; all deserted me. May it not be charged against them!* ¹⁷ *But the Lord stood by me and gave me strength to proclaim the word fully, that all the Gentiles might hear it. So I was rescued from the lion's mouth.* ¹⁸ *The Lord will rescue me from every evil and save me for his heavenly kingdom. To him be the glory for ever and ever. Amen.*

¹⁹ *Greet Prisca and Aquila, and the household of Onesiphorus.* ²⁰ *Erastus remained at Corinth; Trophimus I left ill at Miletus.* ²¹ *Do your best to come before winter. Eubulus sends greetings to you, as do Pudens and Linus and Claudia and all the brethren.* ²² *The Lord be with your spirit. Grace be with you.*

ᵉOther ancient authorities read *Gaul*

In the last part of the work, the personal note, so prominent in ch. 1, and noticeably stronger than in either I Timothy or Titus, increasingly reasserts itself. It has in fact hardly been lost throughout the Epistle. It reaches a climax from v. 6 onwards. More keenly than ever, we are faced with the question of its significance. Many scholars who see these works as pseudonymous believe that in this passage (opinions differ about the extent), if not elsewhere, we have a genuine fragment of Paul's work. It is not that the vocabulary is particularly Pauline; just that the material seems too poignantly personal, placed as it is in writings often regarded as rather flatly impersonal, to be from any other source than Paul himself. But though there is in this chapter a greater concentration of such material than elsewhere, we are inclined to believe that the personal element is no greater here than in other parts of II Timothy and that the writer has deliberately intensified this quality in this section of his three-part composition (cf. p. 19f.).

Further, we do not believe that the personal details in this chapter, more numerous though they are, have been arrived at by means or for reasons different from those at work elsewhere in these writings. Their chief purpose is to give vivid colour to an edifying portrait of Paul the heroic leader of the Church's early days, a model for his successors. That does not necessarily mean that the writer simply invented them arbitrarily – though that may be the right explanation, at least in part. There are signs that some items have a relationship, not as direct as we should find natural, with Paul's undoubted writings. Others may have links with Acts, though it is impossible to be certain what they are or how they may have been formed. A mixed solution may be correct: we have some genuine tradition, and some invention to fill out the picture in the interests of the Pauline cause. Perhaps we are wrong to expend effort in pursuing our natural inclination to salvage at least some direct connection with the pen of Paul himself. This was a period when legend-making was irresistible. Every hero of the early Church (and of course many others besides in other spheres of life in the ancient world) was soon embellished with a wealth of mythical biography. Where tradition lacked names, names were provided. Where events were hazy, outlines were filled in. But the interest here is not so much to provide a complete life or even picture of Paul as to give realism and conviction to the case which has moved the writer to go to work.

1

I charge you etc: cf. I Tim. 5²¹. Here the angels are omitted. But the solemnity is intensified by pointing ahead to the Judgement Day, when Christ will return in glory.

to judge the living and the dead: not only this phrase but also the verb *charge (diamarturomai)* link this passage with Acts 10^{42}. It is one of the more striking connections of wording between our writer and Acts; cf. v. 7 below.

appearing: Greek *epiphaneia,* cf. I Tim. 6^{14}; II Tim. 1^{10}; 4^8; Tit. 2^{13}. Otherwise, in New Testament, only in I Thess. 2^8.

kingdom: in these writings, only here and in v. 18. The Synoptic Gospels show Jesus speaking of the Kingdom of God not only as future but also as present, or imminent, in his ministry; and Paul uses the term sometimes with reference to the present, but often with reference to the coming End and the dispensation which will then ensue (e.g. I Cor. 6$^{9f.}$). The latter is probably true of Acts, e.g. 14^{22}; 28^{23,31}; as it is also here. With the prospect of the coming glory held out from time to time in these writings, the Christian leader is to keep to his task, however long it may be required of him (v. 2).

2

preach: cf. I Tim. 2^7; II Tim. 1^{11}. *The word:* the gospel, the faith.

be urgent: better, 'be on guard'.

3

sound teaching: cf. I Tim. 1^{10} (same Greek).

itching ears: cf. Acts 17^{20}. Both this and the following verse use the Greek *akoē,* lit. 'hearing'. ('Feeling an itch with regard to the hearing'.) cf. I Tim. 1^4 etc.

5

evangelist: only here and in Acts 21^8 and Eph. 4^{11}. An office or function not known to Paul, at least by this title. Perhaps hardly distinguishable from *preacher* (I Tim. 1^7). For *euaggelion, gospel,* that which the evangelist proclaims, cf. II Tim. 1^8.

6–8

In these verses, the apostle makes his most solemn statement, before turning to personalia. Much of it, however, has parallels elsewhere in these writings.

being sacrificed: throughout this letter (though not at all in I Timothy and Titus) it has been clear that 'Paul' is set in prison (1^8; 2^9). Now the poignancy (and so the impressiveness) reaches its height as it is disclosed that he is about to be put to death. This verse is probably modelled on Phil. 2^{17}, which uses the same verb; cf. also Phil. 1^{23}. Apart from the matter of imminent death, the atmosphere of sad farewell is close to that built up in Acts $20^{18ff.}$, Paul's speech to the elders of the Ephesian congregation, a passage which has a number of points of contact with these writings (cf. v. 7 below).

7

the good fight: cf. I Tim. 6^{12} – like master, like servant. The fight in mind is that of the games; cf. *the crown,* v. 8, as well as *the race.* For the Pauline background, cf. I Cor. 9^{24-7}.

finished the race: a possible point of contact with Acts, cf. 20^{24}. The only other use of *dromos (race)* in the New Testament is in another Pauline speech, Acts 13^{25}. As in 3^{11}, the question arises of the direction of the dependence, if any. The options are: genuine Pauline speech and writing; coincidental use of the same imagery; our writer's use of a crucial Pauline speech in Acts; the incorporation by the writer of Acts of what he took to be a vivid Pauline image.

kept the faith: the article probably means that the writer has his usual sense of *faith* (i.e. the Christian faith) in mind; but the phrase, with or without an article, is a common idiom: cf. 'to keep faith'.

8

crown: cf. II Tim. 2^5. *Of righteousness:* i.e. probably, as a reward for righteousness, which, in this writer, is straightforwardly a moral quality, 'uprightness'. The garland, customarily awarded to victors in the games, was also used as a symbol of immortality (cf. 1^{10} and the Polycarp reference, below).

the Lord: i.e. Christ, cf. v. 1.

laid up: perhaps the idea that lists of those victorious are kept in heaven, cf. the idea of the Book of Life, Rev. 21^{27}; Phil. 4^3; and II Tim. 2^{19}. The language used in this verse becomes customary in relation to martyrdom: cf. the Martyrdom of Polycarp, 17, 19 (*ECW*, p. 161f.).

10

Demas: the name is also found in Col. 4 [14] and Philem. [24], in both cases associated with Luke, cf. v. 11.

has deserted: takes up a theme initiated in 1[15]. Unless authentic, this is partly an aspect of the heroic portrait of Paul, partly by way of example to discouraged Christian leaders. *World:* lit. 'age', by contrast with the age to come.

Crescens: no other reference. The margin is to be rejected. *Galatia* is in the writer's mind from his mention of Antioch, Iconium and Lystra in 3[11].

Titus: in the Letter to him, he is associated with Crete, though it is not necessarily implied that he is still there (1[5]). *Dalmatia:* Paul's preaching in Illyricum (made up of Dalmatia and Pannonia) is referred to in Rom. 15[19]. It is seen as the furthest limit of his work, which is perhaps why it is introduced here: in view of the writing of the Letter to Titus, it is hard to suppose that we are meant to see Titus (or Crescens) as having positively deserted Paul. The implication may rather be that from prison, Paul oversees his churches in Asia Minor and the Adriatic coast. That is certainly the atmosphere in Philippians and Colossians, also written from prison, but here, it must be admitted, there is a most un-Pauline atmosphere of arousing pity for Paul in his isolation.

11

Luke alone: but see v. 21 below; which shows the artificiality of the passage. By the time he reaches the conventional greetings, the writer has forgotten the means he used earlier to create the desired effect, and imitates Paul's customary collections of names at the end of his letters.

Luke: only here and in Col. 4[14] and Philem. [24].

Mark: also appears in Col. 4[10] and Philem. [24]. But he also plays a part in Acts (12[12,25]; 15[37,39]) and appears in I Peter 5[13].

useful: Greek *euchrēstos*, cf. Philem. [11]. Mark is reminiscent of Onesimus.

12

Tychicus: cf. Col. 4[7]; Eph. 6[21], where he probably again plays a part in adding authentic Pauline colour to a pseudonymous work. We might

have expected this sentence to have been with the other departures in
v. 10. Our writer seems to have preferred to group together the names
he has, for the most part, derived from Philemon, or perhaps, the later
verses of Col. 4.

13

parchments: Greek *membranai;* a Latin loan-word; probably refers to
parchment leaved notebooks, then coming into fashion in the East; a
Roman invention. *Books:* Greek *biblia;* the more general word, which
might include scrolls.*

14

Alexander: cf. I Tim. 1^{20}. And in Acts 19^{33}, in a confused scene at
Ephesus (in mind from v. 12), in the course of trouble aroused by the
*silver*smiths, a Jew called Alexander comes forward, apparently on
their side. In the same verse, the verb cognate with the noun *apologia*
(defence), cf. v. 16, is used. These phenomena may or may not be
significant: they may point to rather confused dependence on the Acts
passage, comparable to the use of Colossians or Philemon just before.
Or it is conceivable that the story in Acts 19 owes at least some of the
bricks used in its construction to our present passage.

16

my first defence: it is unclear which of Paul's trials as reported in Acts is
in mind here – if indeed any of them. Those who attempt to link these
letters with the life of Paul as known from other sources, his letters and
Acts, and who find themselves compelled to push them into the period
after that covered in those writings, see here a reference to a first trial of
Paul in Rome. But if we are to take a more literary view of these
writings and suppose that the writer has little interest in precise biographical reference, then he is writing in general dependence on
Philippians, as far as statements about the imprisonment are concerned,
and on Colossians and Philemon for many of his names. The word
apologia occurs (though not in the same technical sense) in Phil. 1^{7,16}. It
is not untypical of our writer to take a Pauline statement and make it
more technical and precise (cf. the attitude to scriptural authority in
3^{16}, see p. 128f.). *Deserted:* cf. on v. 10 above.

*See T. C. Skeat in G. W. H. Lampe (ed.), *The Cambridge History of the
Bible,* vol. 2, Cambridge University Press, 1969, ch. 3, especially p. 66.

17

all the Gentiles: probably based on Phil. 1$^{12-14}$, in combination with an allusion to Paul's vocation as apostle to the Gentiles, cf. Gal. 1^{16}.

lion: cf. Psalm 22^{21}. Perhaps figurative, perhaps not.

18

heavenly kingdom: at the parousia of Christ or perhaps after death; cf. v. 1.

the glory etc: cf. I Tim. 1^{17}, p. 61.

19–22

These concluding verses begin with the form of greetings, but are by no means sharply distinguished from the preceding remarks. Colossians has the same character (4$^{10ff.}$), though the section which begins with the first mention of greeting is much longer. The same is true of Romans (16$^{3ff.}$).

Prisca and Aquila: Rom. 16^3 is virtually reproduced in this greeting. According to that passage the couple are in Rome; whereas in I Cor. 16^{19}, they themselves send greetings, apparently from Ephesus, where a congregation meets *in their house.* If this is seen as a difficulty, then it may be resolved by taking Rom. 16 as originally addressed to the church in Ephesus not Rome, a destination to which other elements in that chapter point. See also Acts 18^{2,18,26}.

Onesiphorus: cf. 1^{16}.

Erastus: in Acts 19^{22}, Paul sends an Erastus with Timothy from Ephesus to Macedonia; and in Rom. 16^{23} we read of Erastus the city treasurer of Corinth. A pavement was discovered at Corinth in 1929, with an inscription stating that 'Erastus Procurator Aedile laid this pavement at his own expense' (other readings have also been suggested of the Latin abbreviations which make up the inscription, in particular 'in return for the aedileship' for PRO AED). It dates from the second half of the first century at the earliest. Clearly, 'Erastus' was a man of distinction, whether identification of the two figures is right or not.★

Trophimus: cf. Acts 20^4; 21^{29}, where he is said to be from Ephesus. In the former passage, he is paired with Tychicus, another Asian, i.e. from

★ See P. N. Harrison, *Paulines and Pastorals*, Villiers, 1964, ch. 11.

Ephesus, as a companion of Paul. *Miletus:* like some other features of
this passage, this points to the journey to Jerusalem described in Acts
20f. being fairly recent when this passage was written; so, if Pauline, it
would be a fragment from Paul's imprisonment at Caesarea, Acts 23$^{23f.}$.
The remaining names are otherwise unknown in New Testament
sources. By the late second century, a Linus was listed among the
earliest bishops of Rome. The presence of Latin names does not prove
that the Pastoral Epistles were written in Rome: such names were by
this time common also in the East.

22

The Lord ... spirit: cf. Gal. 6^{18}; Phil. 4^{23}; Philem. ^{25}.

Grace be with you: cf. I Tim. 6^{21}.

The Letter to Titus

¹ *Paul, a servant*ᵃ *of God and an apostle of Jesus Christ, to further the faith of God's elect and their knowledge of the truth which accords with godliness,* ² *in hope of eternal life which God, who never lies, promised ages ago* ³ *and at the proper time manifested in his word through the preaching with which I have been entrusted by command of God our Saviour;*

⁴ *To Titus, my true child in a common faith: grace and peace from God the Father and Christ Jesus our Saviour.*

⁵ *This is why I left you in Crete, that you might amend what was defective, and appoint elders in every town as I directed you,* ⁶ *if any man is blameless, the husband of one wife, and his children are believers and not open to the charge of being profligate or insubordinate.* ⁷ *For a bishop, as God's steward, must be blameless; he must not be arrogant or quick-tempered or a drunkard or violent or greedy for gain,* ⁸ *but hospitable, a lover of goodness, master of himself, upright, holy and self-controlled;* ⁹ *he must hold firm to the sure word as taught, so that he may be able to give instruction in sound doctrine and also to confute those who contradict it.* ¹⁰ *For there are many insubordinate men, empty talkers and deceivers, especially the circumcision party;* ¹¹ *they must be silenced, since they are upsetting whole families by teaching for base gain what they have no right to teach.* ¹² *One of themselves, a prophet of their own, said, 'Cretans are always liars, evil beasts, lazy gluttons'.* ¹³ *This testimony is true. Therefore rebuke them sharply, that they may be sound in the faith,* ¹⁴ *instead of giving heed to Jewish myths or to commands of men who reject the truth.* ¹⁵ *To the pure all things are pure, but to the corrupt and unbelieving nothing is pure; their very minds and consciences are corrupted.* ¹⁶ *They profess to know God, but they deny him by their deeds; they are detestable, disobedient, unfit for any good deed.*

ᵃ*Or slave*

The opening greeting of Titus is much longer (vv. 1–4) and fuller than those of I and II Timothy (cf. p. 45). It is probably right to see it as intended to be an epitome of the writer's teaching: his concept

of the true faith. In this comparatively short work, he finds it desirable
to make such a statement right at the beginning. But Titus is richer,
for its size, in doctrinal passages than its companion pieces: cf. also
2[11-14] and 3[4-7]. In I Timothy we wait until 3[16] for anything comparable, apart from the brief statement in 1[15]. These verses are full of
the writer's key doctrinal words – *truth, godliness, life, preaching,
entrusted.*

The rest of the chapter combines two themes familiar from the
other letters – the qualifications for Christian leaders and the threat
from heresy. Special features of their treatment here are noted below.

1

servant: I and II Timothy have only the commoner *apostle*. But Romans
and Philippians open with this term, whose theological significance
Paul expounds in I Cor. 7[21f.]. Titus combines both *servant* and *apostle*,
cf. Romans 1[1].

to further: this renders the Greek preposition *kata* (lit. 'according to').
It makes this verse parallel to I Tim. 1[1] and II Tim. 1[1], where the same
preposition occurs (with *command* and *promise* respectively). RSV here
is open to serious question. It is more likely that *faith* and *knowledge*
and *hope* are all marks of the apostle which he shares with his people,
cf. NEB: 'marked as such by faith and knowledge and hope – the faith
of God's chosen people, knowledge of the truth as our religion has it,
and the hope of eternal life'. But NEB margin allows the option which
RSV adopts.

elect: cf. II Tim. 2[10].

knowledge of the truth: cf. I Tim. 2[4]; II Tim. 2[25]; 3[7].

godliness: cf. p. 59. The true piety: the word is a little more concrete
in our writer's use of it than *godliness* implies.

2

hope . . . eternal life . . . promised: an extended equivalent of II Tim. 1[1].
Hope itself echoes I Tim. 1[1], where it is centred on Christ.

eternal life: cf. p. 60.

who never lies: the Greek adjective *apseudēs*. Here alone in the New
Testament. But God's faithfulness to his promises and to his people is
a common Pauline theme, cf. especially I Cor. 1⁹; II Cor. 1¹⁸.

ages ago: the same Greek phrase as in II Tim. 1⁹, but here the sense is
more straightforward (cf. p. 112). The idea of the revelation of God's
long-standing purpose (promised in the Old Testament) is prominent
in Paul: cf. Rom. 16²⁵ᶠ· (a passage used before by this writer, cf. p. 112f.);
also I Cor. 2⁷⁻¹⁰. The underlying idea is the same in II Tim. 1⁹ᶠ·.

3
at the proper time: lit. 'in its own time'. Same phrase as in I Tim. 2⁶; 6¹⁵.
The second of these passages is comparable.

manifested: in I Tim. 3¹⁶, it refers to the coming of Christ in the flesh; in
II Tim. 1¹⁰, to the present availability, through Christ's coming, of
God's grace. Here, it is instead *eternal life* which is manifested in God's
word – a parallel scheme. The *word* is the doctrine which has then to be
preached by authorized officers, such as Paul the apostle. *Logos* (*word*) is
also used for *saying* in passages like I Tim. 1¹⁵ and Tit. 3⁸. These doctrinal 'sayings' are parts of the 'word' in the more general sense, the
Christian teaching; cf. also II Tim. 2⁹; and I Tim. 5¹⁷, where it is properly translated *preaching*, the spoken teaching.

have been entrusted: cf. I Tim. 1¹¹.

by command: exactly as in I Tim. 1¹.

Saviour: cf. I Tim. 1¹; p. 47.

4
true child: cf. I Tim. 1².

Grace and peace: two terms only, as in Paul's genuine letters; contrast I
and II Tim.

Christ Jesus our Saviour: cf. II Tim. 1¹⁰; and pp. 47, 113.

5
I left you in Crete: the implied presence of Paul with Titus in Crete
engaged in missionary work finds no confirmation either in Paul's

letters or in Acts, where his only link with the island is during his event-
ful sea journey to Rome described in ch. 27. Though this piece of information may represent genuine history (for Acts is both stylized in its
account of Paul and doubtless incomplete in telling us where he worked,
and the Epistles are fragmentary as sources for data of this kind), it is
hardly worth struggling to 'fit it in'. It is at least equally probable that
this is part of the fictitious framework of these writings. It is an early
stage in the legend-making process which flourished in the second century concerning, among other things, the travels and activities of the
apostles. Why Crete is chosen here is a mystery to us, for it was not, as
far as we know, a Christian centre at this time, certainly not an important one. If we knew more of our writer's situation and interests, no
doubt the matter would be plain.

elders in every town: as in Acts 14²³; an important link between the two
writings. For this title, see p. 75. The system of church government
enjoined here is closer than that in I Timothy to that envisaged in Acts
(so far as this is clear or precise). That is, if this passage thinks in terms
of a ruling group of elders (who may equally have the title 'overseer',
bishop, cf. v. 7, where *for* speaks in favour of taking it thus). But it may
be that, as in I Timothy, the two offices are distinct and the group of
elders has a single bishop at its head – v. 7 has the definite article (which
RSV fails to show). In that case, one purpose of this passage is to complement I Tim. 3, that is to state the moral qualifications for the office
of elders, just as the earlier passage gave the largely identical requirements for bishops and deacons. It remains unclear why they should not
all have been given in one place. The suggestion, aimed at easing the
bishop–elder obscurity here, that vv. 7–9 (as indeed I Tim. 3¹⁻¹³) have
been interpolated in the interests of the episcopal Church order of a
somewhat later period, is a last resort. (Even if here the sense would
flow more smoothly, this is not true of I Tim. 3.) It is better to suppose
that, as in Acts, the exact details of congregational structure were not
fixed and not everywhere identical. Here, even if *the bishop* is distinguished from *the elders,* he seems to be closer to them than in I Timothy.
Whether 'Titus' is to be seen as a 'bishop' is a further element of
obscurity here. It seems more likely that he is the external supervisor
of a number of congregations (cf. p. 110).

as I directed you: even if the precise structure of Church leadership may
not have been a vital matter to our writer, proper authorization certainly was; cf. p. 110.

6

blameless: cf. I Tim. 3^{10}, concerning deacons.

the husband of one wife: cf. I Tim. 3^{2,12}; p. 77.

children are believers: cf. I Tim. 3$^{4f.}$; II Tim. 1^5, for the concept of the Christian family.

7

steward: cf. I Cor. 4^1, for Paul's use of this image. There, the apostle (or perhaps Christians in general) is the steward of God's mysteries. Here the idea may be rather that he cares for God's household (*oikonomos, steward – oikos,* 'house'). Not surprisingly, in this and comparable passages, there is an easy comparison between the congregation and the family (though the former is already formal enough for them to be distinguished, as we see here). Congregations met in the houses of leading members (e.g. Col. 4^{15}), and they must have been so close-knit that they resembled substantial urban households of the period. This may show itself in the general shape of these passages outlining the duties of various groups in the congregation: they closely resemble contemporary manuals for households, which are reflected directly in New Testament passages like Col. 3$^{18ff.}$, cf. p. 78. The related noun *oikonomia* appears in I Tim. 1^4, though probably not with a lively sense of this image in mind.

a drunkard or violent: as in I Tim. 3^3. The previous two adjectives here only.

greedy for gain: as in I Tim. 3^8, concerning deacons.

8

hospitable: cf. I Tim. 3^2.

master of himself: Greek *sōphrōn,* cf. p. 70; I Tim. 3^2.

upright: Greek *dikaios,* the adjective cognate with 'righteousness'.

holy: Greek *hosios,* 'devout'.

self-controlled: Greek *egkratēs,* here alone in the New Testament.

9

sure word: same wording as I Tim. 1^{15} and its parallels, but referring to the teaching as a whole (cf. v. 3 above, p. 141). This verse is an expanded equivalent of the adjective *didaktikos*, 'apt at teaching', used in I Tim. 3^2.

sound doctrine: cf. II Tim. 4^3. The remedy against the heresy to which the writer now turns.

10

empty talkers: the personal noun cognate with that rendered *vain discussion* in I Tim. 1^6.

the circumcision party: cf. v. 14. This is the clearest sign that the heresy in view in these writings is Jewish Christian in origin; but certain features of it have already pointed in that direction, cf. p. 55f. We should suppose, then, that the Cretans specially in mind in v. 12 are Cretan Jews, converted but now gone astray. However, it cannot be said that the Jewishness of the opponents is in any way emphasized and there is indeed a notable absence of a sense that the Jewish question is any longer in the foreground of Church life (cf. p. 36ff.). It may then be the case that, as far as the writer's own time is concerned, the orthodox body's opponents are dissident Christians, some of whose teachings may have had Jewish origins or support, and that this reference is simply part of the Pauline scenario. If so, it is easier to see that any inconsistency with v. 12 (see below) did not trouble our writer. This phrase is characteristic of Paul, cf. Gal. 2^{12}.

11

for base gain: cf. I Tim. 6^5. The repeated use of charges of this kind is an indication that the picture of the heretics is to some degree conventional.

families: cf. II Tim. 3^6.

no right: lit. 'what they must (ought) not'; i.e. because it is false.

12

one of themselves: the line quoted is from Epimenides, a poet of the sixth to fifth century B.C., who was a Cretan but not a Jew; though possibly the giving of the title *prophet* may indicate that our writer thought him so. It is more likely that the word is used in the general sense (cf. John 11^{51} for a man thus 'seized' by God) and alludes to the reputation which the writer had as a sage and diviner. Both Cicero and Aristotle attribute these powers to him.

13

rebuke: Greek *elegchō*, better 'expose'. Same word rendered *confute* in v. 9. The word contains the sense of public rebuttal. They must be seen to be in error.

14

Jewish myths: cf. I Tim. 1^4, p. 55. *Commands:* perhaps Jewish regulations beyond those which coincided with this Church's accepted rules, cf. I Tim. 1^8. It was a major question in the early Church, resolved in various ways in various places, which elements in the Jewish law to retain; cf. e.g. Rom. 13$^{9f.}$; Acts 15^{20}; cf. also Mark 7$^{1-23}$; Matt. 5$^{17-19}$; 23^{3,23}.

15

all things are pure: in view of the reference to Jewish rules, the allusion here is probably to food regulations, and the point is related to that made in I Tim. 4^4. cf. Rom. 14^{20} (also centres on *katharos, pure*); also Lk. 11^{41}. There is no distinction here as in Paul between 'robust' Christians and those of tender conscience (cf. I Cor. 8^7); rather, only that between the orthodox and the heretics. Their consciences are not tender but corrupt. The lines have hardened. Note the play on different senses of *pure*, ritual and moral, applied to things and persons. I Tim. 4^4 gives the theological reason which may motivate the strong condemnation of the ascetics: it is a failure to recognize God as creator. Whether their corruptness consists in more than their differing from the orthodox and refusing their authority (cf. *insubordinate*, v. 10) is not made clear. In II Tim. 3$^{1ff.}$ the writer launches into general condemnation of them on moral grounds. The general idea is a commonplace, with parallels in Seneca and Philo: e.g. from the latter, 'Everything else too that the unclean person touches must be unclean'.*

*Spec. leg., 3, 208, see F. H. Colson (ed.), *Philo*, VII, Heinemann, p. 605.

BY CONTRAST: THE CHRISTIAN
CHARACTER

¹ *But as for you, teach what befits sound doctrine.* ² *Bid the older men be temperate, serious, sensible, sound in faith, in love, and in steadfastness.* ³ *Bid the older women likewise to be reverent in behaviour, not to be slanderers or slaves to drink; they are to teach what is good,* ⁴ *and so train the young women to love their husbands and children,* ⁵ *to be sensible, chaste, domestic, kind, and submissive to their husbands, that the word of God may not be discredited.* ⁶ *Likewise urge the younger men to control themselves.* ⁷ *Show yourself in all respects a model of good deeds, and in your teaching show integrity, gravity,* ⁸ *and sound speech that cannot be censured, so that an opponent may be put to shame, having nothing evil to say of us.* ⁹ *Bid slaves to be submissive to their masters and to give satisfaction in every respect; they are not to be refractory,* ¹⁰ *nor to pilfer, but to show entire and true fidelity, so that in everything they may adorn the doctrine of God our Saviour.*

¹¹ *For the grace of God has appeared for the salvation of all men,* ¹² *training us to renounce irreligion and worldly passions, and to live sober, upright, and godly lives in this world,* ¹³ *awaiting our blessed hope, the appearing of the glory of our great God and Saviour*ᵇ *Jesus Christ,* ¹⁴ *who gave himself for us to redeem us from all iniquity and to purify for himself a people of his own who are zealous for good deeds.* ¹⁵ *Declare these things; exhort and reprove with all authority. Let no one disregard you.*

3 ¹ *Remind them to be submissive to rulers and authorities, to be obedient, to be ready for any honest work,* ² *to speak evil of no one, to avoid quarrelling, to be gentle, and to show perfect courtesy towards all men.* ³ *For we ourselves were once foolish, disobedient, led astray, slaves to various passions and pleasures, passing our days in malice and envy, hated by men and hating one another;* ⁴ *but when the goodness and loving kindness of God our Saviour appeared,* ⁵ *he saved us, not because of deeds done by us in righteousness, but in virtue of his own mercy, by the washing of regeneration and renewal in the Holy Spirit,* ⁶ *which he poured out upon us richly through Jesus Christ our Saviour,* ⁷ *so that we might be justified by his grace and become heirs in hope of eternal life.* ⁸ *The saying is sure.*

*I desire you to insist on these things, so that those who have believed in God may be careful to apply themselves to good deeds*ᶜ; *these are excellent* *and profitable to men.* ⁹ *But avoid stupid controversies, genealogies, dissensions, and quarrels over the law, for they are unprofitable and futile.* ¹⁰ *As for a man who is factious, after admonishing him once or twice, have nothing more to do with him,* ¹¹ *knowing that such a person is perverted and sinful; he is self-condemned.*

ᵇOr *of the great God and our Saviour* ᶜOr *enter honourable occupations*

There is little in this central, hortatory section of Titus which is not in essence to be found in the letters to Timothy – apart from the description of 'our' pre-conversion state in 3³. It completes a pattern familiar to us from the companion writings, adding to the condemnation of heresy a positive statement of the behaviour required within the Christian community. In this case, however, it is dominated by the needs of the Christian household (cf. p. 78f.). Compare similar lists of duties in Col. 3¹⁸ff.; Eph. 5²²ff.; I Peter 2¹⁸ff..

1

sound doctrine: cf. I Tim. 1¹⁰; Tit. 1⁹ etc.

2ff.

In general form these lists of duties are reminiscent of those laid down for the officers of the congregation in ch. 1 (and in I Tim. 3, as well as for widows in I Tim. 5); but in Greek the linguistic form is different – with the verb *einai* ('to be') instead of 'must': 'the old men are to be . . .' etc., perhaps taking up 'it is fitting' from v. 1 and understanding it before the following regulations. In I Tim. 5¹ there is a brief instruction to 'Timothy' about the proper treatment of some of the categories referred to more extensively in this passage.

2

older men: Greek *presbutēs*, a word related to that translated *older man* in I Tim. 5¹, but, more technically, *elder* in Tit. 1⁵ etc. (*presbuteros*, lit. 'older man', cf. p. 92).

temperate: cf. I Tim. 3²,¹¹.

serious: cf. I Tim. 3⁸,¹¹.

sensible: Greek *sōphrōn,* cf. I Tim. 3[2]; Tit. 1[8] (RSV, *master of himself*).

in faith, in love: cf. I Tim. 1[14], p. 59. For the trio, including *steadfastness* (*hupomonē*), I Tim. 6[11] and II Tim. 3[10], where they are among the qualities of the Christian leader and 'Paul' himself, respectively.

3
older women: cf. I Tim. 5.

reverent: lit. 'as befits priests'; cf. I Tim. 2[10] and 5[5] – Christian old women are to be devout women. For the next two qualities, cf. I Tim. 3[11], probably concerning deacons' wives. Repetition, perhaps, because formulas are being used.

teach what is good: that is, to the *young women,* v. 4 (cf. I Tim. 2[12]). The Christian tradition of domestic virtue is transmitted through the female line. The veto on women teaching in I Tim. 2[12] (the Greek makes it almost certain that this is absolute and not just a prohibition on their teaching men) presumably applies to more general doctrinal and moral instruction: that remains in the hands of the Church's male leaders, properly authorized for the purpose.

4f.
train: Greek *sōphronizō,* of the *sōphrōn* family of words; better, 'urge', 'encourage'.

domestic: Greek *oikourgos;* here only in the New Testament. Thoroughly typical. cf. I Tim. 5[14].

submissive: cf. I Tim. 2[11] and I Cor. 14[35]; also Eph. 5[22ff.].

word . . . discredited: cf. I Tim. 6[1]; identical Greek verb.

6ff.
RSV fails to show the connection between v. 6 and what follows. In Greek *show* is a participle, so that the behaviour described in v. 7 is to characterize 'Titus'' exhortation to the *younger men;* but the account of this behaviour then seems to become generalized in v. 8 – unless the younger men were particularly likely to have opponents.

6
control themselves: Greek *sōphronein;* or 'be prudent'.

7

in all respects: this may better be taken with v. 6, to add a little substance to what is otherwise a very bare instruction.

8

nothing evil to say: cf. I Tim. 3^7; 6^1; Tit. 2^5; this writer has a strong concern with reputation. That the Church's good name is of such importance to him is an important pointer to his sense of its place in society. We may compare the writer of Acts, with his persistent determination to show how blameless Christians were in relation to the Roman authorities and how their troubles arose always from Jewish malice.

9f.

slaves: cf. I Tim. $6^{1f.}$; p. 97. Traditional theme of contemporary ethics and traditional material for expressing it; but expressed in line with our writer's particular emphases, at least at the end of v. 10.★

masters: the closely similar passage Col. 3^{22} uses *kurios*, our writer *despotēs*.

God our Saviour: cf. p. 47.

11–14

A doctrinal interlude (cf. 3^{4-8}), mixed with more hortatory material in v. 12. The passage is close to formulations in the other letters, in particular II Tim. $1^{9f.}$. The pattern of discipline springs from God's gracious acts in Christ; at this basic level, then, our writer, here more clearly than anywhere, conforms to the teaching of Paul (as indeed of other New Testament writers).

grace: cf. II Tim. 1^9. *Appeared:* from Greek *epiphainō*, cognate verb with *epiphaneia* (*appearing*), used, as the verb is here, of Christ's first coming in II Tim. 1^{10}. For the same use of the verb, cf. Tit. 3^4. The noun is applied equally to first and second comings (cf. p. 101): emphasis has now shifted sufficiently from the return of Christ at the End for language which Christians no doubt first applied only to that coming event to be equally used of his first appearance in the flesh – seeing the two in balance.

★ cf. J. L. Houlden, *Paul's Letters from Prison*, Penguin, 1970, p. 210ff.

THE LETTER TO TITUS

All men: cf. I Tim. 2⁴; p. 66.

training: Greek *paideuō*. The word occurs also in I Tim. 1²⁰ (the passive
rendered by RSV *learn*) and II Tim. 2²⁵ (RSV *correcting*). It is an important word in the vocabulary of Hellenistic education and family life,
with its strong sense of discipline. This atmosphere has been fully
absorbed by this writer. Paul had used the word as the LXX does, to
mean rather 'chasten' – i.e. involving the idea of salutary punishment,
cf. I Cor. 11³²; II Cor. 6⁹. For our writer, the fruit of God's saving
grace was less a life of sacrificial suffering than a process of disciplined
training (cf. II Tim. 2³ᶠ·).

sober, upright and godly: Greek *sōphrōn, dikaios, eusebēs* – three of our
writer's most highly esteemed qualities.

world: lit. 'age', Greek *aiōn*.

13f.
In these verses the reminiscences of Paul become stronger, as they tend
to do in all this writer's doctrinal passages (though the Pauline sense of
some of the key words tends to be shifted and flattened).

hope: cf. I Tim. 1¹; Tit. 1²; 3⁷. This eschatological motif is stronger in
Titus than in its companions. cf. Rom. 5²; 8²⁴.

appearing: cf. p. 101. *Glory:* cf. I Tim. 1¹¹; II Tim. 2¹⁰.

God and Saviour: at first sight, the translation given in the margin seems
preferable. This writer applies the title *Saviour* to both God and Christ
(cf. Tit. 3⁴ and 3⁶). See p. 47. Though he has a high view of Christ as
exercising the function of God, it may seem unlikely – and, apart from
one reading of I Tim. 3¹⁶ (cf. p. 84), without parallel elsewhere in his
works – that he would call Christ simply *our God*. I Tim. 2⁵ stands
against it. But the Greek certainly yields more easily the translation in
the text. How may it have been intended?
    In these works the future *appearing* (*epiphaneia*) is always that of
Christ. Though God desires men's salvation (I Tim. 2³ᶠ·), Christ always
takes the more dynamic role. He will be manifested, while God remains in the background, when the eschatological drama takes place (cf.
Matt. 25³¹ᶠᶠ·). Like the son of man in Daniel 7 (to take the leading Jewish
source) and, perhaps more significantly for this particular text, like the

deified Roman emperor, Christ will 'appear' in splendour to carry out
the divine imperial functions of judgement and sovereignty. Given his
penchant for the strongly imperial word *epiphaneia* (*great* also belongs
to this religious idiom), it is perhaps in that direction that we should
look for the root of his apparently rather abrupt attribution to Christ
of the title *God*. The writer may have an eye on the world of divinities
in general, the pagan culture which surrounded him, so that we should
translate 'our deity' (i.e. as distinct from other people's). This need not
at all imply recognition of their reality or validity. Parallels in the contemporary Ignatius may be comparable (p. 86).

gave himself: cf. I Tim. 2^6; Gal. 1^4.

redeem: Greek *lutroomai*, cognate with *antilutron* (*ransom*) in I Tim. 2^6,
see p. 68. For the verb, cf. only, in New Testament, Lk. 24^{21}; I Peter
1^{18}. Also Ps. 130 (LXX 129)^8.

iniquity: Greek *anomia*, lit. 'lawlessness'. It may be significant that this
writer, with his sense of organized and disciplined moral life, should
choose this word; cf. I Tim. 1^8.

purify for himself a people of his own: a number of Old Testament passages
lie in the background and have been used here. Chief among them is
Ex. 19^5, a passage used in a similar sense in I Peter 2^9. Deut. 14^2 has the
same phrase, *a people of his own*. For *purify*, and indeed for the idea of
being rescued (Greek *ruomai*) from iniquities (our word here, *anomiai*),
cf. Ezek. 37^{23}. The use of these passages and of this cultic language belongs to a stream of early Christian theology which is not otherwise
prominent in these writings and of which Hebrews is the most concentrated example: that which saw the Church as the new Israel and expressed this by the imagery of the holy people of God, especially as
gathered in the sanctuary for sacrificial worship. The imagery is found
in many New Testament writers, including the Gospel of John and
Paul himself. In particular, for *people* (*laos*), cf. Rom. $9^{25f.}$; $11^{1f.}$. Closer
in atmosphere to our writer is the use of it in the roughly contemporary
I Clement, with which we have found numerous points of comparison;
cf. chs. 41 and 64 (*ECW*, pp. 44, 57).

15
cf. I Tim. 1^{18}. The point is simply to reaffirm the authoritative nature
of the teaching given.

3 1

Remind them: cf. II Tim. 2^{14}, where *them* refers back to *the elect* of v. 10. Here there is no clear group to which it can refer – certainly not the slaves of v. 9f. These are general admonitions to Christians. The phrase may have been simply lifted from the earlier use – if so, it would be a sign that the three writings should be taken as a single literary work.

submissive to rulers: cf. I Tim. 2^2; and, in Paul, Rom. 13$^{1ff.}$. Admonitions on this subject are found in a similar context of lists of Christian duties in I Peter 2$^{13ff.}$.

honest work: the Greek has 'good deed', as in 1^{16}, of which we have here the contrary situation. cf. also v. 14, where there is a stronger case for the alternative sense. Rom. 13^3, in mind from the earlier part of the verse, has the same Greek, in the sense of 'good deed', so confirming our preferred translation.

speak evil: lit. 'blaspheme'. The verb is taken thus in I Tim. 1^{20}; 6^1; Tit. 2^5; and in all but the first case clearly bears that sense.

courtesy towards all men: cf. Gal. 6^{10}.

3–8

A faithful saying: (v. 8), cf. p. 59f.: unlike the others, and unlike other passages which resemble it, this passage begins with a statement of that from which God has given salvation. The only comparable collection of vicious qualities in these writings is to be found II Tim. 3$^{2ff.}$, which lists the characteristics of the heretics (and others). There are a few links with our present catalogue, especially the hating of others. But the chief links are with Paul (or pseudo-Paul) especially Eph. 2^2 and 5^8; also I Cor. 6^{11}. The painting of the contrast between life before and after conversion was becoming a set theme. However, it is notable that the estrangement which has now been removed is here expressed in moral rather than 'status' terms; so though vv. 5 and 7 use the Pauline doctrine of salvation by God's initiative and not man's own works, the idea has hardly been absorbed and the general picture is one of transference from a morally reprehensible state into one which carries the assurance of *eternal life.* Contrast Eph. 2^{12}, though not 2$^{1f.}$.

3

slaves: contrast Rom. 6^{16}, where we read of slavery to sin. The idea of slavery to passions is much more characteristic of the common Hellenistic tradition of moral teaching, owing most to Plato and the Stoics, at this period the major element in the ethical atmosphere of the Hellenistic world, and affecting Jews and Christians alongside everybody else. *Disobedient* may come from the same passage, cf. Rom. 6¹⁷.

pleasures: not found in Paul.

malice and envy: both figure in the list of vices in Rom. 1²⁹, as marks of Gentile society.

hated by men and hating: the Greek does not give the same effect. 'Hateful' is given by *stugētos*, 'hating' by *miseō*.

4
but when: the contrast is stated by reference to the great act of salvation, the coming of Christ. Note that it is the coming, the 'appearing', which is seen as significant. Only in I Tim. 2⁶ and Tit. 2¹⁴ do we find what look like references to Jesus' death, and it is not in the least dwelt upon. For the possible imperial-cult background to this emphasis, cf. p. 101.

loving-kindness: Greek *philanthrōpia*, lit. 'love of men'; so there is a contrast between human hatred and divine love (vv. 3 and 4).

God our Saviour: cf. p. 47. Christ was the manifestation of God's goodness.

5
saved us: cf. p. 60. The use of 'save' in the past tense is not typical of Paul, but it is found in Rom. 8²⁴ and in the pseudo-Pauline Eph. 2⁵,⁸. The rest of the verse is more strongly Pauline than the parallel passage in Tit. 2¹¹⁻¹⁴; cf. v. 7 also. As in II Tim, 1⁹, the doctrine of justification by grace not works is placed side by side with the language of 'epiphany' and the expectation of eternal life. There is no far-reaching attempt to integrate them.

mercy: Paul never uses this word in this kind of context, with regard to this central theological concept. The Pauline contrast is between man's works on the one hand and his faith and God's grace on the other (cf. Rom. 3²⁸; 4¹⁶).

washing of regeneration: cf. Eph. 5^{26} also referring to baptism, the only other use of *loutron (washing)* in the New Testament. *Paliggenesia* (lit. 'rebirth') is used in Matt. 19^{28} to refer to the Last Day, but that is not the reference here. Rather, like *renewal*, it looks to the common religious aspirations of many pagan groups, and has a Christian root in Rom. 6^4. It reads as if it may be a common expression. Note, however, that its ethos here is moral, not ecstatic as it would be in the mystery cults etc.

renewal in the Holy Spirit: the association of the Holy Spirit with baptism goes back to Christian origins; cf. e.g. I Cor. 12^{13}; Matt. 28^{19}. This is the only reference to baptism in these writings, but for the resulting endowment with the Spirit, cf. II Tim. 1^{14}, also Col. 3^{10}.

6

poured out: cf. Joel 2^{28} (used in Acts 2^{18}); and Rom. 5^5.

7

justified by his grace: cf. Rom. $5^{1f.}$; 4^{16}. As we have found before, a passage in Romans seems to provide the model, but its words are split up and rearranged. It would be in line with our writer's strong moral concern if the Pauline language of 'justification' (primarily concerned with man's status before God) concealed the sense of moral uprightness. That was the sense of *dikaiosunē* in v. 5 (as normally in these writings); it is one of his key aspirations (I Tim. 6^{11}; II Tim. 4^8); and he may well mean here 'so that having been made morally upright by his grace we might be...'

heirs: cf. Rom. 8^{17}. The phrase *hope of eternal life* echoes 1^2.

8

I desire: cf. p. 69. *Good deeds:* cf. 2^{14}; $3^{1, 14}$.

9

In familiar terms, we return to the attack on any tendency to have truck with heresy. The verse is an echo of the opening of the writer's case in I Tim. 1^4, where some of the same words are used.

quarrels over the law: cf. I Tim. 1^7 and Tit. 1^{14}.

10

factious: Greek *hairetikos:* formerly used in a good sense ('able to discriminate'). The cognate noun already has a bad sense in Paul (cf. Gal. 5^{20}). Now it is on the edge between 'factious' and 'heretical'.

admonishing: cf. Matt. 18$^{15f.}$. Rom. 16^{17} advocates a somewhat less active policy.

11

'If the person being exhorted still does not listen, error becomes sin' (Dibelius/Conzelmann, p. 151).

3$^{12-15}$ INSTRUCTIONS AND FAREWELLS

^{12} *When I send Artemas or Tychicus to you, do your best to come to me at Nicopolis, for I have decided to spend the winter there.* ^{13} *Do your best to speed Zenas the lawyer and Apollos on their way; see that they lack nothing.* ^{14} *And let our people learn to apply themselves to good deeds^{d}, so as to help cases of urgent need, and not to be unfruitful.*

^{15} *All who are with me send greetings to you. Greet those who love us in the faith. Grace be with you all.*

^{d}Or *enter honourable occupations.*

This passage is comparable to II Tim. 4$^{9ff.}$, but the atmosphere is quite different. No crisis besets Paul. He is not in prison but in Nicopolis (wherever that may be!). He is far from alone. There is no attempt to win sympathy for him or to portray him in heroic colours. Only here in this letter does the situation of 'Paul' become at all apparent.

Yet the content of Titus is almost wholly a reproduction of that of the other two pieces. It is scarcely possible to imagine two such similar works as II Timothy and Titus being written by the Paul of history at such widely separated times as the personalia must presuppose. So either this is a genuine fragment, placed here simply for the sake of providing a morsel of Pauline realism; or it is fictitious, with the same end in view, perhaps deliberately representing Paul in a different situation from II Timothy in order to show him steadfast to his policies in all situations, at all stages of his career, in prosperity as well as adversity.

12
Artemas: here only. *Tychicus:* cf. on II Tim. 4¹²; p. 134.

Nicopolis: there were several towns of this name. That in Epirus is the most likely to be in mind here.

13
Zenas: here only.

lawyer: probably in the secular sense, not the Jewish.

Apollos: one of Paul's leading collaborators, who is nevertheless some-what ill-defined in the Epistles (cf. I Cor. 1¹²; 3⁶), and is not helped by the marginal treatment received in Acts (18²⁴–19¹). Between the lines, he seems to have been one of the chief missionaries of the first genera-tion.

14
See v. 1.

15
love us in the faith: probably a final reference to the solidarity of the orthodox which has been the writer's object throughout.

Grace: cf. I Tim. 6²¹ and II Tim. 4²².

Index of References

THE BIBLE
Old Testament and Apocrypha

New Testament

157

Index of Names

Index of Subjects